The Penguin Poets

Verlaine

Paul Verlaine was born in Metz in 1844 and published his
first book of verse, *Poèmes saturniens*, in 1866. He led a
turbulent life, complicated by an unsatisfactory marriage and
his fascination for the forceful personality of Rimbaud. In
1873 he quarrelled with Rimbaud and shot him, and was
then imprisoned for two years. After his release he returned
to the Catholic faith, and his poem *Sagesse* (1881) resulted
from this period of repentance. Although no longer at the
height of his powers, Verlaine continued to publish books of
verse until his death in Paris in 1896.

Joanna Richardson was educated at St Anne's College,
Oxford, and is a Member of the Council of the Royal
Society of Literature. She has contributed to a number of
literary journals and newspapers, including *The Times*, the
Spectator, the *New Statesman* and the *New York Times Book
Review*. She is a well-known author whose publications
include a number of historical biographies and critical
studies. Her latest works are *La Vie Parisienne 1852–1870*
(1971) and *Enid Starkie* (1973).

Selected Poems

Verlaine

Chosen and translated
with an introduction by
Joanna Richardson

Penguin Books

Penguin Books Ltd, Harmondsworth,
Middlesex, England
Penguin Books Inc., 7110 Ambassador Road,
Baltimore, Maryland 21207, U.S.A.
Penguin Books Australia Ltd, Ringwood,
Victoria, Australia
Penguin Books Canada Ltd,
41 Steelcase Road West, Markham, Ontario, Canada

First published 1974

Copyright © Joanna Richardson, 1974

Made and printed in Great Britain by
Cox & Wyman Ltd,
London, Reading and Fakenham
Set in Monotype Bembo

CONTENTS

*The Roman numerals preceding poem-titles in these pages refer to the
section and poem divisions to be found in the Pléiade edition of
Verlaine's complete works (Librairie Gallimard, 1962).*

CONTENTS

The Roman numerals preceding poem-titles in these pages refer to the section and poem divisions to be found in the Pléiade edition of Verlaine's complete works (Librairie Gallimard, 1962).

Contents

Contents

Contents

INTRODUCTION

Paul-Marie Verlaine was born on 30 March 1844. He was born in Metz, almost on the borders of Luxembourg and Germany. His father, a captain in the engineers, happened to be stationed there. Captain Verlaine came from an old family in the Belgian Ardennes. On the paternal side, Verlaine was therefore Walloon in origin. But though Nicolas-Auguste Verlaine was an irreproachable army officer, it is worth noting that his own father had spent his youth between church and tavern, with occasional bursts of wild behaviour, and that at one point he became an ardent revolutionary. As for the captain's grandfather, he was a hard-drinking waggoner who was once fined six gold florins for blasphemy. From the Verlaines, the future poet inherited alcoholism, violence, originality, and a strong element of piety.

As for his mother, Élisa Dehée, she came from a prosperous Artois family, solid bourgeois, with an affection for the soil. From the Dehées, he inherited his deep-rooted bourgeois instincts and his attachment to a country life.

But Mme Verlaine was thirty-five when her son was born. She had been married for twelve years before, at last, she gave birth to this child. She loved him with the doting love that only such a mother could bestow. Verlaine soon understood that she would give him all he wanted, and that she would forgive him for all his failures. Her tolerance was almost saintly, and yet, perhaps, it led to his undoing. It deprived him of the discipline essential to the child and to the man. It also created the intense relationship between mother and son which is a breeding-ground of homosexuality.

Verlaine's carefree childhood ended in 1851, when the captain resigned his commission. There was clearly no future for him in the army, and, since his wife was well-to-do, they were not dependent on his pay. Besides, if they had ambitions for their only son, it was obvious that they should move to Paris, and that the boy should begin his education. That year they settled in a Parisian suburb, Les Batignolles. Verlaine was seven.

He went to a local boarding-school, and later he attended the classes at the Lycée Bonaparte. His personal development was far from satisfactory. He suffered from the excessive indulgence he received from his family. His mother allowed him – perhaps she wanted him – to remain weak and dependent. From an early age, he was also aware of his remarkable ugliness. Bound to his mother, he understood that he was unlikely to be loved or indulged by other women. It was the classic situation in which a boy would turn to his own sex. At school he had doubtful relationships with several of his friends. He also discovered his love of literature; he read widely, and he began to write poetry.

In 1862 he passed his *baccalauréat*. Then he entered the École de Droit and took a course in arithmetic. He intended to sit for the examination of the Ministry of Finance. Throughout his life he would always keep the inherited instinct to lead a regular, middle-class existence. But he abandoned his studies, and eventually became a copying-clerk at the Hôtel de Ville. He did not deign to rise any higher, although he had had a good education. For he was not only bourgeois, he was bohemian. He preferred a bohemian life; he was intent on writing poetry.

In 1865, he was often seen in the bookshop of Alphonse Lemerre in the passage Choiseul. Lemerre was the publisher of *Le Parnasse contemporain* – an occasional anthology of new poems. The first issue of this publication appeared in March 1866; the eighteenth and last appeared that July. The poets who contributed to the first series – and Verlaine was among them – became known as the Parnassians. The Parnassians – led by Leconte de Lisle – were a group of poets who represented the scientific and positivist spirit of the age. Parnassian poetry was objective, impersonal and restrained; it confined itself to descriptions of nature, remarkable for their static, pictorial quality. It attempted to convey philosophical conceptions. It aimed at formal perfection, and it rejected technical liberties. But while Verlaine wrote his poetic essays in the Parnassian style as a form of literary discipline, he was already drawn, instinctively, to poetry of quite another order.

This was clear from his first book, *Poèmes saturniens*. It was published by Lemerre in 1866. The most remarkable personal influence in this collection is that of Baudelaire. We see it, for example, in the poem 'Crépuscule du soir mystique' – the very title recalls Baudelaire's 'Le Crépuscule du soir'. Already, in his first book, Verlaine's literary debts recall his own saturnine and romantic nature; and already, in his first book, he is writing poems which he alone could have written. Among them is 'Chanson d'automne', which is pure, unadulterated Verlaine. Even now, he has dropped the mask of impassibility; he has brought poetry close to music, not merely in sound, but in its emotional power.

Only three years lay between the publication of *Poèmes saturniens* in 1866 and that of *Fêtes galantes* in 1869; but between the two books lay a chasm. *Poèmes saturniens* had been marked by literary exercises and experiments, and strongly coloured by literary influences. Verlaine had begun to establish himself as a poet of mood. In *Fêtes galantes*, with astonishing suddenness, he showed himself to be a poet of extraordinary technical accomplishment, a poet of exquisite sensibility. He re-created a distinctive world. The fundamental melancholy cannot obscure the brilliance of these tiny verbal pictures, these miniature conversation-pieces and declarations of love. In the twenty-eight poems of *Fêtes galantes*, Verlaine catches and enshrines the world of Watteau. He was to write nothing more delicate than the opening poem, 'Clair de lune'; he wrote nothing more subtle, more intensely evocative than the final poem, 'Colloque sentimental'.

Fêtes galantes was published by Lemerre in July 1869. By the time it appeared, Verlaine's life had changed dramatically. For some time, now, it had become increasingly clear that he needed the stability of marriage. His drinking habits were already grave. He drank enormously – and his drunkenness produced not only intellectual atony but extreme physical violence. He was just twenty-five; he was not indifferent to his disgrace, and at moments he felt profound disgust at his behaviour. He would enter a church – he had pious ancestors – and he would make his confession. He would avoid the temptations of cafés, and show himself to be a model employee at the Hôtel de Ville. Then, once again, heredity and weakness would prevail, and he would succumb to temptation.

In June 1869, he met his future wife. Mathilde Mauté was just sixteen; she lived with her parents in the rue Nicolet, in Montmartre. She was innocent, pretty, snobbish, carefully brought up and genteel. Verlaine met her through one of his friends – her half-brother, Charles de Sivry. He fell in love with her at first sight, and he recalled their meeting in the lines 'En robe grise et verte avec des ruches . . .' The poem appeared in *La Bonne Chanson*. This anthology, inspired by his love for Mathilde, was printed in June 1870 – just before the outbreak of the disastrous Franco–Prussian

War. Among the twenty-one poems were the lines which begin:

> La lune blanche
> Luit dans les bois . . .

It is not surprising that Debussy, Fauré and so many others were to set Verlaine to music.

La Bonne Chanson might be described as Verlaine's wedding-present to his wife. They were married on 11 August 1870. But the marriage was mistaken from the first. It was strained by the war, by the Siege of Paris, and by the Commune. Mathilde was soon pregnant; but her pregnancy did not draw her husband to her. He returned to his drinking habits; and in 1871 he was dismissed – with his colleagues – from the Hôtel de Ville, for suspected Communard sympathies. He had no regular employment. He and Mathilde went to live with her parents in the rue Nicolet. There was small prospect of a happy future. It was at this moment that Arthur Rimbaud wrote to him from Charleville, and asked for his opinion of his poetry.

Verlaine was immensely impressed by the poems Rimbaud sent him, and invited him to come and stay in Paris. Early in September, Rimbaud arrived at the rue Nicolet. He was not quite seventeen.

Verlaine was frustrated and disappointed by marriage, he longed for a relationship which would sweep him out of his bourgeois surroundings, satisfy all his physical and emotional needs. He wanted someone younger than himself, someone whom he could dominate, and yet he wanted someone with a stronger character than his own. Since his marriage, thirteen months earlier, he had tried to live an irreproachable life, but it had sometimes seemed that he was acting a part. Since his marriage he had not satisfied a fundamental need of his nature. He had not written poetry. If he was to write again, this new, irresistible influence was essential. Now there arrived this handsome, ruthless, turbulent young boy, who was also a poet of rare distinction.

A few weeks later, in October 1871, Mathilde gave birth to Georges, Verlaine's son. In May 1872, after savage bursts of drinking, after homicidal attacks on Mathilde, after nearly killing their child, Verlaine left the house. He was enslaved by Rimbaud. They went together to Belgium. Mathilde followed them, in vain, to try to bring him to his senses. But Verlaine found the attraction of Rimbaud overwhelming. Nothing else in his life, which was a life of many passions, ever approached it. The physical attraction was violent and intense, and it was strengthened by poetic kinship, poetic inspiration. Rimbaud swept him into a life of unhoped-for adventure, a life which cast all middle-class morality aside, a life which seemed superbly apart. They were both exalted by their liaison, by their utter liberty, by the poetic prospects before them; and, during their relationship, they touched the heights of poetry. From Belgium they went to London; and there, it seems, Rimbaud began *Les Illuminations*, and Verlaine wrote some of *Romances sans paroles*.

Mathilde was now determined to secure a separation – divorce was not yet legally possible. But it is clear that Verlaine still felt a certain love for her:

> Ô triste, triste était mon âme
> A cause, à cause d'une femme . . .

In his complex mind, he still hoped to return to her; and, somehow, to keep Rimbaud as well.

Romances sans paroles, which many consider to be his finest book, reflects his persistent love for Mathilde; it also bears the ineffaceable mark of Rimbaud. It was Rimbaud whom Verlaine followed as he created an original, unacademic language. Rimbaud advocated pictorial simplicity, a return to popular sources, to simple refrains and simple rhythms. Verlaine followed his guidance, bringing some of his poems close to popular songs, seeking a new simplicity and a new complexity. Just as Rimbaud freed Verlaine from bourgeois domesticity, from suburban mediocrity, so he shook him free from certain literary conventions, and swept him into a splendid adventure: the search for a new poetry. In some ways, Rimbaud was only appealing to instincts and beliefs which were already present: to Verlaine's sympathy for the simple and the popular, to his love of technical experiments, his lifelong pleasure in exploring and exploiting language and syntax, his interest in expressing moods. Verlaine was already a supreme poet of mood; under Rimbaud's influence he attempted to eliminate himself from his work, to record mood and atmosphere without the intervention of self. This was the ultimate refinement of poetry.

On 10 July 1873, both men were back in Brussels; Verlaine was now obsessed with the thought that Rimbaud was going to leave him. In a moment of drunken passion, he shot him. Rimbaud was only slightly wounded, but Verlaine was arrested. The prison doctors declared that he showed signs of recent homosexual relations. The medical report was irrelevant to the charge of criminal assault, and modern doctors do not consider that the evidence produced was reliable. However, the report was read in court, and the judge imposed the maximum penalty. Verlaine was sentenced to a fine of 200 francs, and to two years' hard labour.

He seems to have been intensely relieved to escape from the violent emotional problems, the ever-present temptations of the world. He had always needed to be ruled; and now an inevitable discipline was imposed on him. In the calm and austerity of his prison life, he was also free to turn in upon himself, to examine his emotions, to question his beliefs, and to express and lose himself in poetry. Inspiration came to him, now, diverse and intense. As he looked between the bars of his prison window in Brussels, he conceived one of his most famous poems:

> Le ciel est, par-dessus le toit,
> Si bleu, si calme!...

And, again in his Brussels cell, he wrote 'Kaléidoscope'. As the title suggests, it is a collection of impressions, with no logical connection. Here, before Proust, Verlaine experiences those rare, mysterious, transient moments which have more savour than the actual events which they revive. The setting of the poem cannot be identified. In the last verse, he destroys any lingering vestige of reality, and leaves the whole poem, suspended, in a dream. Like certain poems by Rimbaud, 'Kaléidoscope' catches a world beyond the world. It is in this sort of poem that Verlaine shows the extent of his powers.

In April 1874, Mathilde obtained her judicial separation, and she was given custody of her child. The prison governor took a copy of the decree to Verlaine – who was finishing his sentence at Mons. Verlaine recorded that he wept; an hour or two later, he asked that the prison chaplain should come to him. Under the stress of emotion, he returned to the Catholic faith, and became the poet of *Sagesse*.

The profound charm of *Sagesse* lies in its obsession with the past. Verlaine's contrition is frail, but it intensifies the forbidden pleasures of the past, the enduring obsession with Rimbaud. When he wrote *Sagesse*, he honestly believed that he had entered the path of salvation; he had been tempted, but determined that he would not now turn back. But one must distinguish between the man's intentions and the very depth of his soul, which he could not help revealing in

poetry. The essential reality is not edifying. There are a few mo-
ments in *Sagesse* when the convert bathes in the purifying love of
Christ; and there are many times when he re-lives and regrets
the forbidden past. Verlaine was not a hypocrite – but *Sagesse*
presents the two contestants in the unequal fight which God
would lose.

Verlaine was released from prison in January 1875. He had served
only eighteen months of his sentence, but the law allowed remission
for prisoners in solitary confinement. He wanted, now, above all, to
avoid the temptations of Paris; he wanted to find himself again, to
lead a respectable life. He decided to teach French in England. Late
in March he arrived in Stickney, a remote Lincolnshire village, to
teach French and drawing at the local school.

He was now especially susceptible to religious influences, and, in
this pious Victorian world, he discovered *Hymns Ancient and Modern*.
He also read *A Pilgrim's Progress*. We may find their influence in his
work. Living in the Poet Laureate's native Lincolnshire, he was,
moreover, drawn to Tennyson – to the stern morality shown in the
Idylls of the King, to the melancholy moods so like his own. In 1876
he moved from Stickney to Bournemouth, where he taught French
and Latin at a Catholic school. He was still working intensely at his
poetry. In October 1877 he returned to France, to teach at the
Collège Notre-Dame at Rethel.

He was still determined to lead an upright life. He was touchingly
determined to be correct. He was still attempting to be reconciled
with Mathilde. But she was understandably adamant. In 1879, when
his hopes were finally destroyed, he succumbed again to drink. He
also fell in love with one of his pupils, Lucien Létinois.

> Cette adoption de toi pour mon enfant,
> Puisque l'on m'avait volé mon fils réel,
> Elle n'était pas dans les conseils du ciel,
> Je me le suis dit, en pleurant, bien souvent . . .

So Verlaine was to lament in *Amour*. In 1879 he left Rethel, and
brought Lucien to England. Lucien taught, briefly, at the school at
Stickney; Verlaine himself took a post at a school in Lymington. It
was, one suspects, that Christmas, in London, that he dropped his
paternal mask and revealed the true nature of his feelings. Soon
afterwards he and his protégé returned to France, where they made
an unsuccessful attempt to farm together. In 1883, at the age of

twenty-three, Lucien died of typhoid. Verlaine was to commemorate him in 'Lucien Létinois', a sequence of poems in *Amour*. The comparison with Tennyson's *In Memoriam* is inevitable, but Verlaine does not benefit from the comparative study. 'Lucien Létinois' remains a personal lament, a private elegy which is not dignified into a long and honest search for faith. No one could have drawn comfort or wisdom from it, or found in it the loftiness of spirit, the poetic richness of Tennyson's work.

Lucien's death coincided with another tragedy in Verlaine's life. He had tried to be reinstated as a municipal employee, but his record in Paris and Brussels remained against him, and he was rejected. This rejection determined his future. He found himself cast into a life of misery. In 1885 he moved into a hideous slum in Paris. For the rest of his days he was to live in penury and squalor – and, by some irony, his status was to be increasingly recognized. In 1884, in the collection *Jadis et Naguère*, his 'Art poétique' made its impact on the literary world. In 1889, in *Parallèlement*, he included 'Laeti et Errabundi', the poem which had been inspired by the rumour of Rimbaud's death. Lucien Létinois was forgotten. Now, as he knowingly faced his decline, Verlaine looked back on his years with Rimbaud as the supreme experience of his past. Rimbaud had been the paramount intellectual influence in his life; he remained the man he transcendently loved.

Verlaine spent his final years in the cafés and hospitals of Paris. Perpetual drinking and squalid living, illness and disease, had made him, now, a wreck of a human being. His homosexual days were virtually over, but he was torn between two middle-aged women of dubious morals, and for one of them he wrote *Le Livre posthume*. Here, for a brief moment, his poetic gift returned. But, for the most part, he turned out sadly pedestrian verse; his inspiration had gone, and he was living on his past. His past now brought its late reward: he lectured in Holland, Belgium and England. In 1894, on the death of Leconte de Lisle, he was elected Prince of Poets.

He died on 8 January 1896 in a two-room apartment in the rue Descartes, in a working-class quarter of Paris. His personal property, it was said, consisted of '5 clay pipes and one cherry-wood pipe – his favourite – a plaster cigarette-holder, two pairs of pince-nez, a pair of shoes and a cotton cap, and . . . that is all'. It was all except his poetry. Literary Paris paid him unheard-of homage at his funeral. A few days later, Edmond de Goncourt noted the fanaticism of the young, who were 'ready to consecrate Verlaine as the greatest poet of the century'.

*

The main themes of Verlaine criticism were already forming. That same month, in *Le Figaro*, Émile Zola enlarged on the theme of Verlaine, the man apart. Far from Verlaine as he had been in his literary principles and his achievement, he spoke of him with admiring sympathy, and with vehement conviction.

Sad, delightful Verlaine has gone to the land of great eternal peace, and already a legend is growing over his grave.

He was, we are told, a solitary, disdainful of the crowd, a man who lived in the lofty dream of his work, without any kind of concession or compromise ... This is quite untrue ... Verlaine did not disdain society, it was society which rejected him. He became an unwilling creature apart, an involuntary 'exile' ... Indeed, so little did he spurn honours and distinctions that, quite seriously, he wanted to stand for the Académie ... If he refused everything, as they have said, that was because nothing was offered him ...

And who knows if misery did not diminish him? Of course the fatal negligence of his life helped to give his poetry that freedom of movement which is its original contribution to literature. But ... I should like to imagine him happy, well off, comfortable, an Academician, having had the leisure to produce all his fruit, like the tree which a kindly destiny shelters from the onslaughts of frost and wind. Certainly he would have left a more complete and more extensive work.

The critic Charles Le Goffic disagreed with Zola: he considered that Verlaine had been genuinely indifferent to honours, and that he had chosen independence. Independent he had certainly been; he had always stood apart, and, as Le Goffic emphasized, the years had not changed him.

Until the end he lived outside the rules of prosody and behaviour. And this independent bohemianism was neither an attitude nor the accepted consequence of his errors: he could (and some have tried to make him do so) make honourable amends, conform to the outward conventions of bourgeois life. He preferred to die his old vagabond self, indifferent to status and to official celebrity: he was honestly uninterested. At the height of his glory he remained a good soul, he broke with none of those he had known in his days of ill-fortune, and he refused to discriminate. He is a singularly *déclassé* figure ... But this *déclassé* had a humble heart; this unnatural Catholic made the sweetest gesture of submissive and repentant piety before the Blessed Virgin; this poet found in the delights of a fallen angel some lines of mortal beauty. His art was great enough, and controlled enough, to efface itself, and to break the bounds of a confining prosody until it became a light and volatile music, a tremor and a cry. There it was that he set himself apart from other poets, and there it is that he remains inimitable and the most wonderful example of the helotism of genius to present to lettered youth in every age.

Some critics insisted that Verlaine had been a perpetual child; others acclaimed him as 'the dear father of us all, a good old grandfather ... In him,' wrote one, 'we proudly honour the great French Christian poet'. Verlaine remained controversial; but now, by common consent, he had entered into glory. It was decided to erect a memorial in the Jardin du Luxembourg; Mallarmé and Rodin presided over the memorial committee. In 1897, the year after Verlaine's death, Mallarmé declared: 'We know that he is smiling in immortality, and that he is now beside La Fontaine and Lamartine'. Verlaine must indeed have been smiling. At the Académie française, José-Maria de Heredia, the Parnassian poet, was singing his praises. In Brussels, Émile Verhaeren proclaimed the greatness of 'the wandering Lélian, whose thumping and imperious stick seems like a symbol on the paths of literature'.

Verhaeren was among Verlaine's most understanding admirers. That April, in *La Revue blanche*, there appeared the generous appreciation which was to be reprinted in his *Impressions*:

After the death of Victor Hugo, it was the death of Verlaine which afflicted French literature most deeply ... Whatever the worth of Banville and Leconte de Lisle, they seem to be tributaries; they do not shine enough with a personal fire ...

Paul Verlaine proves himself to be quite different. If the *Poèmes saturniens* are still impregnated with Parnassian traditions, if the *Fêtes galantes* seem to derive from 'La Fête chez Thérèse', which Victor Hugo arranged in his *Contemplations*, the *Romances sans paroles* and, above all, *Sagesse*, affirm their independence in French literature. These works are no longer subjects, they are sovereigns. They live with a new and special art ...

Verlaine never knew calm ... His being is always shaken by anguish or pacified by prayer; he is always burning with vices, or with virtues ... He is a man as profoundly as he is a Christian. And it is his double nature that, as a great poet, he has sung, expressed and immortalized ...

He spiritualized the language; he was tempted by shades of meaning, and by the fragility of phrases. He composed some which were exquisite, fluid, tenuous.

They seem scarcely a tremor in the air; the sound of a flute in the shadows in the moonlight; the vanishing of a silk dress in the wind; the trembling of glass and crystal on a dresser. Sometimes all that they contain is the docile gesture of two hands coming together . . .

It will be the original glory of Paul Verlaine to have conceived, lived and created a work of art which, alone, reflects and enlarges the rebirth of faith – that rebirth which we have seen in recent years . . .

There are moralists who reproach Verlaine for his dissipated and sinful life. One really wonders if it should be deplored, as soon as one recalls the cries of repentance, of gentleness, humility and sacrifice with which he redeemed it.

Other critics were less admiring and less charitable. A psychiatrist, discussing decadent poetry, considered that 'Verlaine was a disturbed man of genius, a progenerate rather than a degenerate, but he had strange deviations and strange weaknesses . . . One is too well aware of the sick man behind the poet.' Several critics confused their moral and aesthetic judgements. In his study *What is Art?*, Tolstoy wrote, in puritan mood:

I cannot refrain from dwelling on the extraordinary glory of these two men, Baudelaire and Verlaine, who are recognized today, throughout Europe, as the greatest geniuses of modern poetry. How can the French . . . attribute such vast importance, and accord such enormous glory, to these two poets, who are so imperfect in manner and so vulgar and so low in matter? . . . The only explanation which I can see is this: that the art of the society in which they produce their works is not something serious and important, but a mere amusement . . .

Baudelaire and Verlaine have invented new forms, they have, moreover, spiced them with pornographic details which nobody before them had deigned to use. And that was all that was needed to make them acknowledged as great writers by the critics and the upper classes.

Despite Tolstoy's moral strictures and left-wing criticism, it was clear that Verlaine now enjoyed a European reputation. In 1899, Georges Rodenbach, the Belgian Symbolist poet, declared that Verlaine's conversion had been 'a struggle between Jesus and a childlike Pascal. And in this sublime crisis were born the eternal poems of *Sagesse*, the most moving confession of the soul in all modern literature'. Rodenbach maintained his belief in Verlaine's immortality. His faith was shared by the publisher who, in 1899–1900, brought out the five volumes of Verlaine's *Œuvres complètes* (followed, in 1903, by his *Œuvres posthumes*). Achille Segard, who had known Verlaine, declared that he had 'established a new form of sensibility, and in it . . . a whole generation rediscovered, enlarged and clarified, the very image of its common soul'. Ernest Raynaud, the historian of Symbolism, wrote that he understood 'all the phenomena of modern neurasthenia . . . No one translated, better than Verlaine, the atrophy which comes from excessive activity, excessive nervous tension, the abuse of life and its stimulants. In his poetry, the apotheosis of transient sensation, Verlaine contrived to catch the indiscernible.'

As the twentieth century began, the familiar trend in Verlaine criticism continued. While men of letters recognized his individual gifts and his influence, the more conventional critics continued to take a moral stand and to show a violent personal resistance to his work. Now that it was no longer possible to ignore Verlaine, people denied his genius with fury. One remains astonished by the tone of the discussion, the degree of anger and invective which sober writers allowed themselves to show. In 1901, René Doumic reviewed his *Œuvres complètes* in the *Revue des deux mondes*.

We have been invited to do something which few of us had done: to read Verlaine in his entirety. This reading . . . makes us appreciate the equal banality of the man and of his work. And so it could not be recommended too warmly to literary novices who would take their elders' word and be tempted to believe in Verlaine's genius. This reading will prevent them from being, in their turn, the victims of a kind of gigantic joke and the dupes of an insolent mystification . . .

Far from being a beginning, the art of Verlaine is the last convulsion of a dying poetry. This poetry is merely Romanticism which has lost its vigour . . . One had only to see Verlaine ambling round the streets to think of the old Romantics in the days of the Bousingots, who were proud to go around the town in clothes which made them noticed, and believed that eccentric dress possessed some secret virtue. The careful disorder and the contrived irregularity of this costume is simply another form of dandyism. Verlaine knew it and he was prepared to admit it. He was not unaware that decent dress would make him lose much of his personality . . .

Verlaine is the frantic representative of intimate poetry thus conceived in conformity with the *credo* of Romanticism. One could not mention any work in which the self has so far been displayed with such boastful cynicism.

It is to be feared that one day Verlaine will be completely forgotten. He has collected his admirers, some of them men of good faith. His poetry has found an echo in certain souls which therefore saw in it something of themselves. This example will be quoted to show into what deliquescence moral ideas and artistic feelings have, at a certain date and in a certain group, very nearly dissolved, lost themselves and foundered.

The controversy and the determined publicity continued. In 1907 Edmond Lepelletier published his biography *Paul Verlaine*. He had been the poet's schoolfriend, and his only claim to fame was this one friendship. His account of Verlaine was sometimes excessively loyal, but it said much that no one else could say, and it roused the former Mme Verlaine to write *Mémoires de ma vie*. Middle-aged, divorced from her second husband, keeping a *pension de famille* in Nice, Mathilde was proud, now, that she had once been praised by a great poet; she was also a little vain that she had been the unfortunate heroine of the drama which remained the strangest adventure in her life. One can only be grateful that she determined to correct and complete Lepelletier's work by her own account of events.

The year 1911 saw, at last, the official recognition of Verlaine. On 28 May his monument was unveiled in the Jardin du Luxembourg. His admirers had waited fifteen years for this moment: fifteen years full of obstacles and intrigues, of continual battles against prejudice. Now the Senate formally accepted his memorial. Rémy de Gourmont, long ago, had written the last words: 'The attacks of the pious and the pedantic had broken against a plinth already as enduring as granite. In his marble beard, Verlaine smiled at eternity, with the air of a Faun who hears the peal of bells.'

*

As a poet, he had done service to modern literature. He had restored the free use of metre, given back to poets the unfettered use of their instrument of work. He had deliberately broken every rule of prosody. He had used his marvellous technical powers, as well as his instincts, to record suggestion. No one else catches, like Verlaine, the infinitely fragile state between dreaming and waking, between imagination and reality. He expresses a thought before it is formulated, an instinct before it is recognized, an emotion which has yet to be acknowledged. As Fernand Gregh observed: 'In many short poems, which are like the tremors of a soul, caught as they pass, it is hardly Verlaine who is talking any more, it is the human soul, impersonal, intemporal, it is almost the soul of things gaining awareness of itself in the soul of a man.' No French poet has recorded certain moods with the exquisite touch of Verlaine. Simple in word and form, he seems to write almost without effort. In their own inherent melody, in their emotive power, his lyrics come as close as any poems have ever come to music.

As a poet of love, he is uneven. As a religious poet, he has perhaps been over-estimated. But 'l'art, mes enfants, c'est d'être absolument ois-même'. So he had explained. No poet had been more himself than Verlaine. He recorded all his life, all his raptures and regrets, all his bitterness, licentiousness and melancholy, all his humour, violence, weakness and simplicity. Verlaine's was at times a subtle simplicity. It was that of a child. It was also that of a consummate poet.

*

In his most characteristic poems, his most subtle evocations of mood, it is almost impossible to translate him. Every word has its depth of association, every syllable its considered music. Even a comparable poet could not approach him. All one can do is to present as faithful a translation as possible, and hope that it may keep some literary virtue.

I have sometimes chosen to translate into free verse; I have usually tried to keep the rhyme scheme of the original. The text is that of the Pléiade edition (Librairie Gallimard, 1962), with the exception of a few minor corrections of obvious printers' errors. The poems are largely taken from Verlaine's earlier collections, because his gifts declined so sharply in his later work. I have, I hope, included most of his celebrated poems; I have also included less familiar and less accomplished ones to complete the likeness of the poet and to suggest the range of his experience and his achievement.

JOANNA RICHARDSON

Poèmes saturniens 1866

MELANCHOLIA

Nevermore

Souvenir, souvenir, que me veux-tu? L'automne
Faisait voler la grive à travers l'air atone,
Et le soleil dardait un rayon monotone
Sur le bois jaunissant où la bise détone.

Nous étions seul à seule et marchions en rêvant,
Elle et moi, les cheveux et la pensée au vent.
Soudain, tournant vers moi son regard émouvant:
«Quel fut ton plus beau jour?» fit sa voix d'or vivant,

Sa voix douce et sonore, au frais timbre angélique.
Un sourire discret lui donna la réplique,
Et je baisai sa main blanche, dévotement.

– Ah! les premières fleurs, qu'elles sont parfumées!
Et qu'il bruit avec un murmure charmant
Le premier *oui* qui sort de lèvres bien-aimées!

MELANCHOLIA

Nevermore

Memory, oh memory, what do you want with me?
Autumn sent the thrush on wings through the unsparkling sky,
And the melancholic sun shone in monotony
On yellow woods where winds roar icily.

We were alone and, in a dream, walked on,
She and I, wild-haired, in liberation.
Then she looked at me in touching question,
Asked: 'Which was your finest day?' in her golden tone,

Her sweet and sonorous voice, cool angelic sound.
With a shy smile I made her understand,
And I kissed her white hand, piously.

– Oh, the first flowers, how they fill the air!
And how the word whispers enchantingly,
The first *yes* that we hear from lips most dear!

Après trois ans

Ayant poussé la porte étroite qui chancelle,
Je me suis promené dans le petit jardin
Qu'éclairait doucement le soleil du matin,
Pailletant chaque fleur d'une humide étincelle.

Rien n'a changé. J'ai tout revu: l'humble tonnelle
De vigne folle avec les chaises de rotin . . .
Le jet d'eau fait toujours son murmure argentin
Et le vieux tremble sa plainte sempiternelle.

Les roses comme avant palpitent; comme avant,
Les grands lys orgueilleux se balancent au vent.
Chaque alouette qui va et vient m'est connue.

Même j'ai retrouvé debout la Velléda
Dont le plâtre s'écaille au bout de l'avenue,
– Grêle, parmi l'odeur fade du réséda.

Three Years Afterwards

I pushed the narrow and unsteady gate,
And in the little garden I walked leisurely.
The morning sun shone on it pleasantly,
And on each flower a dewy spangle set.

Nothing has changed: the arbour covered yet
With vines, the rattan chairs of memory . . .
The fountain murmurs on as silverly,
The aspen sighs perpetual regret.

The roses flutter to remind; and, to remind,
The great proud lilies balance in the wind.
Each lark which comes and goes is known to me.

I found the Velleda still standing there,
Its plaster flaking, by the shrubbery,
– Fragile. Faint mignonette hung in the air.

Vœu

Ah ! les oaristys ! les premières maîtresses !
L'or des cheveux, l'azur des yeux, la fleur des chairs,
Et puis, parmi l'odeur des corps jeunes et chers,
La spontanéité craintive des caresses !

Sont-elles assez loin toutes ces allégresses
Et toutes ces candeurs ! Hélas ! toutes devers
Le printemps des regrets ont fui les noirs hivers
De mes ennuis, de mes dégoûts, de mes détresses !

Si que me voilà seul à présent, morne et seul,
Morne et désespéré, plus glacé qu'un aïeul,
Et tel qu'un orphelin pauvre sans sœur aînée.

Ô la femme à l'amour câlin et réchauffant,
Douce, pensive et brune, et jamais étonnée,
Et qui parfois vous baise au front, comme un enfant !

Wish

Oh! the oaristys! the first mistresses!
The bloom of flesh, the blue of eyes, the gold of hair,
And, in the fragrance of young bodies fair,
Caresses timidly spontaneous!

Is it not distant, now, that happiness
And all that candour! Oh, it has gone far!
Springs of regret have fled my winters sore
Of discontent, of tedium and distress!

So here I am alone, dismal, alone,
Dismal, forlorn, more cold than an old man,
Poor orphan, with no older sister blessed.

Oh woman with her love reviving, mild,
Gentle, brown-haired and pensive, unsurprised,
Who sometimes kissed your forehead, like a child!

Mon rêve familier

Je fais souvent ce rêve étrange et pénétrant
D'une femme inconnue, et que j'aime, et qui m'aime,
Et qui n'est, chaque fois, ni tout à fait la même
Ni tout à fait une autre, et m'aime et me comprend.

Car elle me comprend, et mon cœur, transparent
Pour elle seule, hélas ! cesse d'être un problème
Pour elle seule, et les moiteurs de mon front blême,
Elle seule les sait rafraîchir, en pleurant.

Est-elle brune, blonde ou rousse ? – Je l'ignore.
Son nom ? Je me souviens qu'il est doux et sonore
Comme ceux des aimés que la Vie exila.

Son regard est pareil au regard des statues,
Et pour sa voix, lointaine, et calme, et grave, elle a
L'inflexion des voix chères qui se sont tues.

My Familiar Dream

I often have this strange, impressive dream
About an unknown woman, whom I love.
She loves me, and, each time, she's not the same
Nor wholly different, and she understands.

She understands me, and my heart is clear
To her alone, alas! explicable
To her alone. The sweat on my pale brow,
She only can refresh it with her tears.

Is she red-haired or fair? I do not know.
Her name? I know it's sonorous and sweet
Like those of people we have loved, now dead.

She gazes in the way that statues gaze,
And in her voice, distant and calm and grave,
Lies the inflexion of dear voices stilled.

L'Angoisse

Nature, rien de toi ne m'émeut, ni les champs
Nourriciers, ni l'écho vermeil des pastorales
Siciliennes, ni les pompes aurorales,
Ni la solennité dolente des couchants.

Je ris de l'Art, je ris de l'Homme aussi, des chants,
Des vers, des temples grecs et des tours en spirales
Qu'étirent dans le ciel vide les cathédrales,
Et je vois du même œil les bons et les méchants.

Je ne crois pas en Dieu, j'abjure et je renie
Toute pensée, et quant à la vieille ironie,
L'Amour, je voudrais bien que l'on ne m'en parlât plus.

Lasse de vivre, ayant peur de mourir, pareille
Au brick perdu, jouet du flux et du reflux,
Mon âme pour d'affreux naufrages appareille.

Anguish

Nothing in you, Nature, touches me:
The fields that feed, the pink reflection
Of pastorals Sicilian, the grand dawn,
The sad solemnity of setting suns.

I laugh at Art, I laugh at Man, at songs,
At poems, temples Greek, the spiral towers
Which the cathedrals stretch into the void,
I look alike on evil and on good.

I have no faith in God, and I renounce
All thought; as for that ancient irony
Called Love, I want to hear no more of it.

Weary of life, and yet afraid of death,
Like the lost brig, the toy of ebb and flow,
My soul prepares for shipwrecks terrible.

PAYSAGES TRISTES

Soleils couchants

Une aube affaiblie
Verse par les champs
La mélancolie
Des soleils couchants.
La mélancolie
Berce de doux chants
Mon cœur qui s'oublie
Aux soleils couchants.
Et d'étranges rêves,
Comme des soleils
Couchants sur les grèves,
Fantômes vermeils,
Défilent sans trêves,
Défilent, pareils
A des grands soleils
Couchants sur les grèves.

MELANCHOLY LANDSCAPES

Sunsets

A faint dawn sky
Casts on the plains
The melancholy
Of setting suns.
The melancholy
Lulls with sweet songs
My heart that dies
In setting suns.
And dreams most strange
Like suns that set
On wild champaigns,
Ghosts roseate,
Unceasing range,
Are ranging yet:
Great suns that set
On wild champaigns.

Crépuscule du soir mystique

Le Souvenir avec le Crépuscule
Rougeoie et tremble à l'ardent horizon
De l'Espérance en flamme qui recule
Et s'agrandit ainsi qu'une cloison
Mystérieuse où mainte floraison
– Dahlia, lys, tulipe et renoncule –
S'élance autour d'un treillis, et circule
Parmi la maladive exhalaison
De parfums lourds et chauds, dont le poison
– Dahlia, lys, tulipe et renoncule –
Noyant mes sens, mon âme et ma raison,
Mêle dans une immense pâmoison
Le Souvenir avec le Crépuscule.

Mystic Twilight

My recollection with the Setting Sun
Reddens and trembles in the ardent sky
Of Hope afire; and, strange partition,
Withdraws and widens in infinity,
And flowers blossom there abundantly
– Dahlia, lily, tulip, snapdragon –
And spring up round a trellis; it moves on
Through the hot exhalation of decay,
The sultry odour of morbidity
– Dahlia, lily, tulip, snapdragon –
Drowning my senses, soul, sagacity,
It mingles in vast swooning ecstasy
My Recollection and the Setting Sun.

Chanson d'automne

Les sanglots longs
Des violons
   De l'automne
Blessent mon cœur
D'une langueur
   Monotone.

Tout suffocant
Et blême, quand
   Sonne l'heure,
Je me souviens
Des jours anciens
   Et je pleure;

Et je m'en vais
Au vent mauvais
   Qui m'emporte
Deçà, delà,
Pareil à la
   Feuille morte.

Autumn Song

The long sobbing
Of violins
  On autumn days
My heart doth wound
And I despond
  Unbearably.

All words are gone.
Sallow and wan,
  When the moment nears,
I then recall
Time's funeral
  And I shed tears;

It is my end,
And the rough wind
  Bears me, in grief,
This way and that,
Precipitate,
  Like a dead leaf.

L'heure du berger

La lune est rouge au brumeux horizon;
Dans un brouillard qui danse la prairie
S'endort fumeuse, et la grenouille crie
Par les joncs verts où circule un frisson;

Les fleurs des eaux referment leurs corolles;
Des peupliers profilent aux lointains,
Droits et serrés, leurs spectres incertains;
Vers les buissons errent les lucioles;

Les chats-huants s'éveillent, et sans bruit
Rament l'air noir avec leurs ailes lourdes,
Et le zénith s'emplit de lueurs sourdes.
Blanche, Vénus émerge, et c'est la Nuit.

Lovers' Time

The moon lies roseate upon the mist;
The meadow falls asleep in dancing haze,
In trails of smoking vapours, and the frog
Croaks in green rushes where a tremor moves.

The water-lilies slowly close again;
Far, far away, in serried silhouettes,
The poplars stand, erect and spectre-thin;
And round about the thickets fireflies roam.

Wood-owls awaken now, and soundlessly
Drag at the black air with their heavy wings.
The zenith fills with secret glimmerings.
Venus emerges, shining. It is night.

Le Rossignol

Comme un vol criard d'oiseaux en émoi,
Tous mes souvenirs s'abattent sur moi,
S'abattent parmi le feuillage jaune
De mon cœur miroitant son tronc plié d'aune
Au tain violet de l'eau des Regrets
Qui mélancoliquement coule auprès,
S'abattent, et puis la rumeur mauvaise
Qu'une brise moite en montant apaise,
S'éteint par degrés dans l'arbre, si bien
Qu'au bout d'un instant on n'entend plus rien,
Plus rien que la voix célébrant l'Absente,
Plus rien que la voix – ô si languissante ! –
De l'oiseau qui fut mon Premier Amour,
Et qui chante encor comme au premier jour ;
Et, dans la splendeur triste d'une lune
Se levant blafarde et solennelle, une
Nuit mélancolique et lourde d'été,
Pleine de silence et d'obscurité,
Berce sur l'azur qu'un vent doux effleure
L'arbre qui frissonne et l'oiseau qui pleure.

The Nightingale

Like frightened birds, in shrill cacophony,
My recollections all swoop down on me,
Swoop down among the yellow foliage
Of my poor heart, which sees its alder-trunk
Bent in the violet water of Regrets
Which, mournful, like quicksilver, flows along,
Swoop down, and then the turbulent uproar,
Now quietened by a damp and rising wind,
Grows slowly still among the leaves, indeed
A moment later you hear nothing more,
Only the voice praising the Absent One,
Only the voice – but oh, how languishing! –
Of the same bird that once was my First Love,
And sings still as it did on the first day;
And in the mournful splendour of a moon
That rises in the heavens, solemn, wan,
A heavy, melancholy summer's night,
A night of silence and obscurity,
Lulls on the sky blown by a gentle wind,
The tree that trembles and the bird that weeps.

CAPRICES

Femme et chatte

Elle jouait avec sa chatte,
Et c'était merveille de voir
La main blanche et la blanche patte
S'ébattre dans l'ombre du soir.

Elle cachait – la scélérate ! –
Sous ses mitaines de fil noir
Ses meurtriers ongles d'agate,
Coupants et clairs comme un rasoir.

L'autre aussi faisait la sucrée
Et rentrait sa griffe acérée,
Mais le diable n'y perdait rien . . .

Et dans le boudoir où, sonore,
Tintait son rire aérien,
Brillaient quatre points de phosphore.

CAPRICES

Woman and Cat

She was playing with her cat,
And it was wonderful to see
The white hand and the paw so white
In twilight at their revelry.

She was hiding – criminal! –
Beneath her mittens of black thread
Her lethal agate fingernails
As sharp and bright as razorblades.

The other also looked demure
And drew in its cutting claws,
But, devilish, she saw it all . . .

And in the room where, sonorous,
Rang out her laughter aerial,
There shone four spots of phosphorous.

SÉRÉNADE

Comme la voix d'un mort qui chanterait
　　Du fond de sa fosse,
Maîtresse, entends monter vers ton retrait
　　Ma voix aigre et fausse.

Ouvre ton âme et ton oreille au son
　　De ma mandoline:
Pour toi j'ai fait, pour toi, cette chanson
　　Cruelle et câline.

Je chanterai tes yeux d'or et d'onyx,
　　Purs de toutes ombres,
Puis le Léthé de ton sein, puis le Styx
　　De tes cheveux sombres.

Comme la voix d'un mort qui chanterait
　　Du fond de sa fosse,
Maîtresse, entends monter vers ton retrait
　　Ma voix aigre et fausse.

Puis je louerai beaucoup, comme il convient,
　　Cette chair bénie
Dont le parfum opulent me revient
　　Les nuits d'insomnie.

Et pour finir, je dirai le baiser
　　De ta lèvre rouge,
Et ta douceur à me martyriser,
　　– Mon Ange ! – ma Gouge !

Ouvre ton âme et ton oreille au son
　　De ma mandoline:
Pour toi j'ai fait, pour toi, cette chanson
　　Cruelle et câline.

SERENADE

Like the voice of a dead man singing
    From deep in his tomb,
Mistress, hear my voice rising:
    Harsh, out of tune.

Your soul and your ears must listen
    To my mandoline:
For you, only, this song is written,
    Loving, obscene.

I'll sing of your eyes, gold and onyx,
    No shadows there,
Then the Lethe of your breast, then the Styx
    Of your sombre hair.

Like the voice of a dead man singing
    From deep in his tomb,
Mistress, hear my voice rising:
    Harsh, out of tune.

Then I'll venerate, as becomes me,
    That flesh marble-white
Whose scent comes back to me, sultry,
    On sleepless nights.

And, at last, I'll speak of your kisses,
    Your scarlet mouth,
And your torturing embraces,
    Angel uncouth!

Your soul and your ears must listen
    To my mandoline:
For you, only, this song is written,
    Loving, obscene.

UN DAHLIA

Courtisane au sein dur, à l'œil opaque et brun
S'ouvrant avec lenteur comme celui d'un bœuf,
Ton grand torse reluit ainsi qu'un marbre neuf.

Fleur grasse et riche, autour de toi ne flotte aucun
Arome, et la beauté sereine de ton corps
Déroule, mate, ses impeccables accords.

Tu ne sens même pas la chair, ce goût qu'au moins
Exhalent celles-là qui vont fanant les foins,
Et tu trônes, Idole insensible à l'encens.

— Ainsi, le Dahlia, roi vêtu de splendeur,
Élève sans orgueil sa tête sans odeur,
Irritant au milieu des jasmins agaçants !

A DAHLIA

Courtesan with hard heart, opaque brown eyes,
Like an ox's eyes, languidly opening,
Your great breast like new marble glistening!

Rich, heavy flower, no fragrance round you lies,
And your body, imperturbably beautiful,
Dull, shows its harmonies impeccable.

You do not even smell of sweat, the smell
Exhaled at least by women in the fields.
Idol, you reign, heedless of sacrifice.

– So does the Dahlia, king in splendour clad,
Raise without vanity its scentless head,
Provoking, while the jessamines entice.

NEVERMORE

Allons, mon pauvre cœur, allons, *mon vieux complice*,
Redresse et peins à neuf tous tes arcs triomphaux;
Brûle un encens ranci sur tes autels d'or faux;
Sème de fleurs les bords béants du précipice;
Allons, mon pauvre cœur, allons, *mon vieux complice!*

Pousse à Dieu ton cantique, ô chantre rajeuni;
Entonne, orgue enroué, des *Te Deum* splendides;
Vieillard prématuré, mets du fard sur tes rides;
Couvre-toi de tapis mordorés, mur jauni;
Pousse à Dieu ton cantique, ô chantre rajeuni.

Sonnez, grelots; sonnez, clochettes; sonnez, cloches!
Car mon rêve impossible a pris corps, et je l'ai
Entre mes bras pressé: le Bonheur, cet ailé
Voyageur qui de l'Homme évite les approches,
– Sonnez, grelots; sonnez, clochettes; sonnez, cloches!

Le Bonheur a marché côte à côte avec moi;
Mais la FATALITÉ ne connaît point de trêve:
Le ver est dans le fruit, le réveil dans le rêve,
Et le remords est dans l'amour: telle est la loi.
– Le Bonheur a marché côte à côte avec moi.

NEVERMORE

Come, my poor heart, *my old accomplice*, come!
All your triumphal arches raise, restore;
Burn rancid incense, with mock prayers adore;
Disguise with flowers the precipice of doom;
Come, my poor heart, *my old accomplice*, come!

Send God your hymn, o chorister grown young;
You, rusty organ, fine *Te Deums* sound;
Rouge your worn cheeks, senile and moribund;
Discoloured wall, with tapestries be hung;
Send God your hymn, o chorister grown young.

Ring, bells, and little bells, and church bells, ring!
Because my dream impossible came true,
And I embraced it; Happiness, who knew
How, every time, to cheat Man's reckoning,
– Ring, bells, and little bells, and church bells, ring!

Happiness walked side by side with me;
But there is no rest for FATALITY:
Worms are in fruit, and truth in reverie,
Remorse in love, for such is the decree.
– Happiness walked side by side with me.

Fêtes galantes   1869

CLAIR DE LUNE

Votre âme est un paysage choisi
Que vont charmant masques et bergamasques
Jouant du luth et dansant et quasi
Tristes sous leurs déguisements fantasques.

Tout en chantant sur le mode mineur
L'amour vainqueur et la vie opportune,
Ils n'ont pas l'air de croire à leur bonheur
Et leur chanson se mêle au clair de lune,

Au calme clair de lune triste et beau,
Qui fait rêver les oiseaux dans les arbres
Et sangloter d'extase les jets d'eau,
Les grands jets d'eau svelts parmi les marbres.

MOONLIGHT

Your soul's a countryside extraordinary
Where masks and bergomasks enchanting roam,
Playing the lute and dancing, melancholy,
Under wild disguises quite unknown.

Although they're singing in a minor key
Of love triumphant and life opportune,
They do not seem to feel felicity,
Their song fades in the brightness of the moon,

The moonlight calm and sad and beautiful,
Which sets the birds a-dream on branches high;
Tall fountains sob with passion over-full,
And marble statues see their ecstasy.

SUR L'HERBE

L'abbé divague. – Et toi, marquis,
Tu mets de travers ta perruque.
– Ce vieux vin de Chypre est exquis
Moins, Camargo, que votre nuque.

– Ma flamme . . . – Do, mi, sol, la, si.
– L'abbé, ta noirceur se dévoile.
– Que je meure, mesdames, si
Je ne vous décroche une étoile!

– Je voudrais être petit chien!
– Embrassons nos bergères, l'une
Après l'autre. – Messieurs! eh bien?
– Do, mi, sol. – Hé! bonsoir, la Lune!

ON THE GRASS

The abbé's rambling. – Let me tell
You, Marquis, that your wig's askew.
– This Cyprus wine's delectable,
Camargo, but less so than you.

– My jewel! . . . Do, re, mi, fa, sol.
– Abbé, your blackness comes to light!
– May I die, Ladies, if for you
I don't unhook a star tonight!

– I'd like to be a puppy, then!
– Let's kiss our shepherdesses one
By one. – I pray you, Gentlemen!
– Do, re, mi! – Ah, good evening, Moon!

L'ALLÉE

Fardée et peinte comme au temps des bergeries,
Frêle parmi les nœuds énormes de rubans,
Elle passe, sous les ramures assombries,
Dans l'allée où verdit la mousse des vieux bancs,
Avec mille façons et mille afféteries
Qu'on garde d'ordinaire aux perruches chéries.
Sa longue robe à queue est bleue, et l'éventail
Qu'elle froisse en ses doigts fluets aux larges bagues
S'égaie en des sujets érotiques, si vagues
Qu'elle sourit, tout en rêvant, à maint détail.
– Blonde en somme. Le nez mignon avec la bouche
Incarnadine, grasse et divine d'orgueil
Inconscient. – D'ailleurs, plus fine que la mouche
Qui ravive l'éclat un peu niais de l'œil.

THE PATH

Painted and rouged as in the pastorals,
Fragile among the enormous ribbon bows,
She passes under the branches crepuscule,
Down the path where, on the old benches, the green moss grows,
With a thousand affectations trivial
Which one usually keeps for some pet animal.
Her long dress, with a train, is blue, the fan
She rumples in slim fingers with large rings
Has erotic pictures, gay in colouring;
She smiles at many a detail, and dreams on.
– Blonde on the whole. A tiny nose, a mouth
Incarnadine, fat and divine with unconscious pride,
– And finer, one might add, than the beauty spot
Which enlivens the silly brightness of the eyes.

A LA PROMENADE

Le ciel si pâle et les arbres si grêles
Semblent sourire à nos costumes clairs
Qui vont flottant légers, avec des airs
De nonchalance et des mouvements d'ailes.

Et le vent doux ride l'humble bassin,
Et la lueur du soleil qu'atténue
L'ombre des bas tilleuls de l'avenue
Nous parvient bleue et mourante à dessein.

Trompeurs exquis et coquettes charmantes,
Cœurs tendres, mais affranchis du serment,
Nous devisons délicieusement,
Et les amants lutinent les amantes,

De qui la main imperceptible sait
Parfois donner un soufflet, qu'on échange
Contre un baiser sur l'extrême phalange
Du petit doigt, et comme la chose est

Immensément excessive et farouche,
On est puni par un regard très sec,
Lequel contraste, au demeurant, avec
La moue assez clémente de la bouche.

PROMENADE

The sky so colourless, the trees so thin
Seem to be smiling at our vivid dress
Which flutters light and casual on the breeze,
Stirred, sometimes, with a movement as of wings.

The gentle wind ruffles the little pool;
Attenuated sunlight, pale and wan
In the low shade of lindens down the path
Reaches us, blue, in death intentional.

Charming coquettes, deceivers debonair,
Tender, but free from declaration,
We revel in our conversation,
And the lovers tease their ladies fair,

Who, sometimes, with hand imperceptible,
Will box the gallant's ear, and then receive
A kiss on the little finger; you conceive
That, as the whole thing's hypocritical,

Enormously excessive, wildly fierce,
One's punished by a very cold, hard glance,
Which loses some of its significance
When one sees how gently lips will purse.

LES COQUILLAGES

Chaque coquillage incrusté
Dans la grotte où nous nous aimâmes
A sa particularité.

L'un a la pourpre de nos âmes
Dérobée au sang de nos cœurs
Quand je brûle et quand tu t'enflammes;

Cet autre affecte tes langueurs
Et tes pâleurs alors que, lasse,
Tu m'en veux de mes yeux moqueurs;

Celui-ci contrefait la grâce
De ton oreille, et celui-là
Ta nuque rose, courte et grasse;

Mais un, entre autres, me troubla.

THE SHELLS

Every incrusted shell
In the grotto where we loved
Does a character reveal.

One our souls' vermilion shows,
Stolen from our hearts' excess
When I'm afire and you're aglow;

Another feigns your languidness
And pallor when, in weariness,
You're angered by my mocking eyes;

This one counterfeits the grace
Of your small ear, and that's a simile
Of your short nape in its fat rosiness;

But one, among the rest, has troubled me.

LE FAUNE

Un vieux faune de terre cuite
Rit au centre des boulingrins,
Présageant sans doute une suite
Mauvaise à ces instants sereins

Qui m'ont conduit et t'ont conduite,
Mélancoliques pèlerins,
Jusqu'à cette heure dont la fuite
Tournoie au son des tambourins.

THE FAUN

An ancient terracotta faun
Laughs in the heart of the green grass,
No doubt foretelling ill will come
After these hours of peacefulness

Which have led both you and me
– Pilgrims of unhappy mien –
Up to this time that passes by,
Spinning, to the sound of tambourines.

A CLYMÈNE

Mystiques barcarolles,
Romances sans paroles,
Chère, puisque tes yeux,
   Couleur des cieux,

Puisque ta voix, étrange
Vision qui dérange
Et trouble l'horizon
   De ma raison,

Puisque l'arome insigne
De ta pâleur de cygne,
Et puisque la candeur
   De ton odeur,

Ah! puisque tout ton être,
Musique qui pénètre,
Nimbes d'anges défunts,
   Tons et parfums,

A, sur d'almes cadences,
En ses correspondances
Induit mon cœur subtil,
   Ainsi soit-il!

TO CLYMENE

Mystical serenades,
Songs without words,
Love, since your eyes,
    Coloured like skies,

Since your voice, passing strange
Vision, doth change
And trouble the view
    My reason knew,

Since your stirring perfume,
Pale as a swan,
Since the white intense
    Of your incense,

Since your whole being,
Insidious song,
Light of angels gone,
    Perfumes and tones,

Has, in sweet cadences,
And correspondences,
Led my subtle heart,
    Then so be it!

L'AMOUR PAR TERRE

Le vent de l'autre nuit a jeté bas l'Amour
Qui, dans le coin le plus mystérieux du parc,
Souriait en bandant malignement son arc,
Et dont l'aspect nous fit tant songer tout un jour !

Le vent de l'autre nuit l'a jeté bas ! Le marbre
Au souffle du matin tournoie, épars. C'est triste
De voir le piédestal, où le nom de l'artiste
Se lit péniblement parmi l'ombre d'un arbre,

Oh ! c'est triste de voir debout le piédestal
Tout seul ! Et des pensers mélancoliques vont
Et viennent dans mon rêve où le chagrin profond
Évoque un avenir solitaire et fatal.

Oh ! c'est triste ! – Et toi-même, est-ce pas ? es touchée
D'un si dolent tableau, bien que ton œil frivole
S'amuse au papillon de pourpre et d'or qui vole
Au-dessus des débris dont l'allée est jonchée.

LOVE LIES FALLEN

The wind the other night cast Cupid down.
In the most secret corner of the park
He smiled, maliciously, and bent his arc:
His look had made us pensive all day long!

The wind the other night cast Cupid down!
The marble scatters in the morning breeze.
It's sad to see the plinth, shadowed by trees
So dark the sculptor's name is almost gone.

Oh! it is sad to see the plinth alone,
And standing by itself! My sombre thoughts
Now come and go in dreams with sorrow fraught,
Predicting years of solitude and doom.

Oh, it's sad! And you, too, I think, feel melancholy
At such a grievous sight, though your roving eye
Delights in the gold-and-purple butterfly
Flitting over the path where the fragments lie.

EN SOURDINE

Calmes dans le demi-jour
Que les branches hautes font,
Pénétrons bien notre amour
De ce silence profond.

Fondons nos âmes, nos cœurs
Et nos sens extasiés,
Parmi les vagues langueurs
Des pins et des arbousiers.

Ferme tes yeux à demi,
Croise tes bras sur ton sein,
Et de ton cœur endormi
Chasse à jamais tout dessein.

Laissons-nous persuader
Au souffle berceur et doux,
Qui vient à tes pieds rider
Les ondes de gazon roux.

Et quand, solennel, le soir
Des chênes noirs tombera,
Voix de notre désespoir,
Le rossignol chantera.

MUTED

Calm in the twilight made
By the leaves high above,
Oh, with this peace profound
Let us suffuse our love.

Let us pour soul and heart,
Senses in ecstasies,
Into their shades inert,
Pines and arbutuses.

Half-close your sleepy eyes,
Fold your arms on your breast,
And from your heart dismiss
All dreams that you possessed.

Let us be satisfied
By the sweet lulling wind
Blowing the russet tide
Of the grass where you stand.

And when the solemn night
Of the black oaks shall fall,
Voice of our sorry plight,
We'll hear the nightingale.

COLLOQUE SENTIMENTAL

Dans le vieux parc solitaire et glacé,
Deux formes ont tout à l'heure passé.

Leurs yeux sont morts et leurs lèvres sont molles,
Et l'on entend à peine leurs paroles.

Dans le vieux parc solitaire et glacé,
Deux spectres ont évoqué le passé.

– Te souvient-il de notre extase ancienne?
– Pourquoi voulez-vous donc qu'il m'en souvienne?

– Ton cœur bat-il toujours à mon seul nom?
Toujours vois-tu mon âme en rêve? – Non.

– Ah! les beaux jours de bonheur indicible
Où nous joignions nos bouches! – C'est possible.

– Qu'il était bleu, le ciel, et grand, l'espoir!
– L'espoir a fui, vaincu, vers le ciel noir.

Tels ils marchaient dans les avoines folles,
Et la nuit seule entendit leurs paroles.

SENTIMENTAL CONVERSATION

In the old lonely park, across the snow,
Two figures passed a little while ago.

Their eyes were lifeless and their lips were dead,
And one could hardly hear the words they said.

In the old lonely park, across the snow,
Two ghosts recalled the days of long ago.

'Do you remember our old ecstasy?'
'Why do you think it should occur to me?'

'Love, does your heart still beat my name to know?
Do you still dream about my spirit?' 'No.'

'Oh the fine days of wordless ecstasy
When we kissed one another!' 'Possibly.'

'How blue the heavens were, how hopes ran high!'
'Hope fled, defeated, to a sombre sky.'

And so, through the wild oats, they walked ahead,
And only darkness heard the words they said.

La Bonne Chanson   1870

«LE SOLEIL DU MATIN
DOUCEMENT CHAUFFE
ET DORE...»

Le soleil du matin doucement chauffe et dore
Les seigles et les blés tout humides encore,
Et l'azur a gardé sa fraîcheur de la nuit.
L'on sort sans autre but que de sortir; on suit,
Le long de la rivière aux vagues herbes jaunes,
Un chemin de gazon que bordent de vieux aunes.
L'air est vif. Par moment un oiseau qui vole avec
Quelque fruit de la haie ou quelque paille au bec,
Et son reflet dans l'eau survit à son passage.
C'est tout.
        Mais le songeur aime ce paysage
Dont la claire douceur a soudain caressé
Son rêve de bonheur adorable, et bercé
Le souvenir charmant de cette jeune fille,
Blanche apparition qui chante et qui scintille,
Dont rêve le poète et que l'homme chérit,
Évoquant en ses vœux dont peut-être on sourit
La Compagne qu'enfin il a trouvée, et l'âme
Que son âme depuis toujours pleure et réclame.

'THE MORNING SUN SERENELY WARMS AND GILDS...'

The morning sun serenely warms and gilds
The rye and corn still damp in dewy fields,
The sky has kept the freshness of the night.
One wanders out just for the sake of it,
Beside the river with dim yellow weeds,
Along a grass path edged by alder-trees.
The air is sharp. At times a bird will soar,
Bearing some honey from the hedge, or straw,
And its reflection lingers, when it's gone.
That's all.
        But it delights the pensive man,
For, bright and gentle, with a swift caress
It's stirred his dream of wondrous happiness,
Recalled a girl, the charming vision,
The white and sparkling apparition
The poet dreams of, and the man holds dear,
Invoking in his prayers, though some may sneer,
The Spouse he has found at last, the soul adored
Which, from the first, his soul has mourned, implored.

«EN ROBE GRISE ET VERTE AVEC DES RUCHES...»

En robe grise et verte avec des ruches,
Un jour de juin que j'étais soucieux,
Elle apparut souriante à mes yeux
Qui l'admiraient sans redouter d'embûches;

Elle alla, vint, revint, s'assit, parla,
Légère et grave, ironique, attendrie:
Et je sentais en mon âme assombrie
Comme un joyeux reflet de tout cela;

Sa voix, étant de la musique fine,
Accompagnait délicieusement
L'esprit sans fiel de son babil charmant
Où la gaîté d'un cœur bon se devine.

Aussi soudain fus-je, après le semblant
D'une révolte aussitôt étouffée,
Au plein pouvoir de la petite Fée
Que depuis lors je supplie en tremblant.

'WEARING A DRESS WITH FRILLS, IN GREY AND GREEN...'

Wearing a dress with frills, in grey and green,
One day in June, when I was full of care,
She entered, smiling, and I feared no snare,
But looked at her with admiration;

She came and went, came back, and spoke to me,
Frivolous, tender, grave, ironical:
And in my darkened soul I seemed to feel
A bright reflection of her company;

Her voice, so delicate and musical,
Accompanied in charming harmony
Her unmalicious wit, her gaiety,
Her babble – a kind heart beneath it all.

And suddenly, after some vague pretence
At a revolt, immediately quelled,
I was by the small Fairy quite enthralled.
Since then, I've prayed to her with reverence.

«PUISQUE L'AUBE GRANDIT, PUISQUE VOICI L'AURORE...»

Puisque l'aube grandit, puisque voici l'aurore,
Puisque, après m'avoir fui longtemps, l'espoir veut bien
Revoler devers moi qui l'appelle et l'implore,
Puisque tout ce bonheur veut bien être le mien,

C'en est fait à présent des funestes pensées,
C'en est fait des mauvais rêves, ah ! c'en est fait
Surtout de l'ironie et des lèvres pincées
Et des mots où l'esprit sans l'âme triomphait.

Arrière aussi les poings crispés et la colère
A propos des méchants et des sots rencontrés ;
Arrière la rancune abominable ! arrière
L'oubli qu'on cherche en des breuvages exécrés !

Car je veux, maintenant qu'un Être de lumière
A dans ma nuit profonde émis cette clarté
D'une amour à la fois immortelle et première,
De par la grâce, le sourire et la bonté,

Je veux, guidé par vous, beaux yeux aux flammes douces,
Par toi conduit, ô main où tremblera ma main,
Marcher droit, que ce soit par des sentiers de mousses
Ou que rocs et cailloux encombrent le chemin ;

Oui, je veux marcher droit et calme dans la Vie,
Vers le but où le sort dirigera mes pas,
Sans violence, sans remords et sans envie :
Ce sera le devoir heureux aux gais combats.

'SINCE DAY IS BREAKING,
SINCE THE DAWN IS HERE...

Since day is breaking, since the dawn is here,
Since, having long escaped me, hope decides,
Invoked, entreated, to wing through the air,
Since all this happiness with me abides:

Forgotten, now, are melancholy thoughts,
Forgotten, wretched dreams – and, best of all,
Forgotten are pursed lips, and irony,
And words where wit might win, but not the soul.

Gone are the clenched fists, and the anger shown
About the rascals and the fools I've met;
Gone, hateful malice! And you, too, are gone,
Oh, cursed glass which helped me to forget!

Now that a Being of the light
Has, in my utter night, the brightness shed
Of love both everlasting and first-born,
By grace, by radiance and goodness bred,

Guided by you, fine eyes with gentle fires,
Led by the hand which holds my trembling hand,
I'll follow the straight path, through mossy ways
Or through the boulder-strewn and desert land;

Yes, I shall walk through life assured, serene,
Towards my destination heavensent,
Feeling no envy, violence or remorse,
In happy duty, in gay tournament.

Et comme, pour bercer les lenteurs de la route,
Je chanterai des airs ingénus, je me dis
Qu'elle m'écoutera sans déplaisir sans doute;
Et vraiment je ne veux pas d'autre Paradis.

And when the tedium of my road is eased
By some old artless song, I can surmise
That she will surely hear me, undispleased;
Indeed I want no other Paradise.

«AVANT QUE TU NE T'EN AILLES...»

Avant que tu ne t'en ailles,
Pâle étoile du matin,
   – Mille cailles
Chantent, chantent dans le thym. –

Tourne devers le poète,
Dont les yeux sont pleins d'amour;
   – L'alouette
Monte au ciel avec le jour. –

Tourne ton regard que noie
L'aurore dans son azur;
   – Quelle joie
Parmi les champs de blé mûr! –

Puis fais luire ma pensée
Là-bas, – bien loin, oh, bien loin!
   – La rosée
Gaîment brille sur le foin. –

Dans le doux rêve où s'agite
Ma mie endormie encor ...
   – Vite, vite,
Car voici le soleil d'or.

'BEFORE YOUR BRIGHTNESS PALES...'

Before your brightness pales,
Star of the morning time,
  – A thousand quails
Sing, sing amidst the thyme. –

Look in the poet's face:
His eyes are full of love,
  – The lark in space
Soars with the dawn above. –

Turn your gaze, vanished now
In the blue light of morn;
  – What joy doth blow
Through fields of ripening corn! –

Then make my reverie
Shine there, – far, far away!
  – The dew doth lie
Bright-gleaming on the hay. –

In dreams in which she's lost,
My love, my sleeping one . . .
  – Make haste, make haste,
For here's the golden sun.

«LA LUNE BLANCHE...»

La lune blanche
Luit dans les bois;
De chaque branche
Part une voix
Sous la ramée ...

Ô bien-aimée.

L'étang reflète,
Profond miroir,
La silhouette
Du saule noir
Où le vent pleure ...

Rêvons: c'est l'heure.

Un vaste et tendre
Apaisement
Semble descendre
Du firmament
Que l'astre irise ...

C'est l'heure exquise.

'THE SILVER MOON...'

The silver moon
Shines in the trees;
Each branch sends down
Words on the breeze:
Green orison . . .

Beloved one.

The pool reflects,
Mirror profound,
The silhouettes
Where willows bend.
The wind sheds tears . . .

Dream, it's the hour.

A loving, vast
Serenity
Descends at last
From starlit sky,
From rainbow-dome . . .

Heaven is come.

«UNE SAINTE EN SON AURÉOLE...»

Une Sainte en son auréole,
Une Châtelaine en sa tour,
Tout ce que contient la parole
Humaine de grâce et d'amour;

La note d'or que fait entendre
Un cor dans le lointain des bois,
Mariée à la fierté tendre
Des nobles Dames d'autrefois;

Avec cela le charme insigne
D'un frais sourire triomphant
Éclos dans des candeurs de cygne
Et des rougeurs de femme-enfant;

Des aspects nacrés, blancs et roses,
Un doux accord patricien:
Je vois, j'entends toutes ces choses
Dans son nom Carlovingien.

'A SAINT IN BLAZE
OF GLORY . . .'

A Saint in blaze of glory,
A Maid in tower above,
All that man can signify
In words of grace and love;

The golden echo of a horn
In forests far away,
The loving, tender pride once known
In Ladies of nobility;

With that the memorable charm
Of a fresh, triumphant smile
That lights the whiteness of a swan,
The blushes of a woman-child;

A look of white and pink, and pearl,
Sweet harmony patrician:
I can see and hear them all
In her name Carlovingian.

«LA DURE ÉPREUVE
VA FINIR...»

La dure épreuve va finir:
Mon cœur, souris à l'avenir.

Ils sont passés les jours d'alarmes
Où j'étais triste jusqu'aux larmes.

Ne suppute plus les instants,
Mon âme, encore un peu de temps.

J'ai lu les paroles amères
Et banni les sombres chimères.

Mes yeux exilés de la voir
De par un douloureux devoir,

Mon oreille avide d'entendre
Les notes d'or de sa voix tendre,

Tout mon être et tout mon amour
Acclament le bienheureux jour

Où, seul rêve et seule pensée,
Me reviendra la fiancée!

'THE HARSH ORDEAL IS GOING TO END...'

The harsh ordeal is going to end:
My heart, smile at the future kind.

Now it is past, the time of fears
When I was wretched even to tears.

Don't calculate the moments still;
Be patient, soul, a little while.

I have read the message grim
And banished every sombre dream.

My eyes, exiled from seeing her
When grievous duty did deter,

My ears, avid to hear her voice,
Its golden notes, its tenderness,

All my love and all my soul
Acclaim the day most wonderful

When, my one dream and reverie,
My sweetheart will return to me!

«VA, CHANSON, À TIRE-D'AILE...»

Va, chanson, à tire-d'aile
Au-devant d'elle, et dis-lui
Bien que dans mon cœur fidèle
Un rayon joyeux a lui,

Dissipant, lumière sainte,
Ces ténèbres de l'amour:
Méfiance, doute, crainte,
Et que voici le grand jour!

Longtemps craintive et muette,
Entendez-vous? la gaîté,
Comme une vive alouette,
Dans le ciel clair a chanté.

Va donc, chanson ingénue,
Et que, sans nul regret vain,
Elle soit la bienvenue
Celle qui revient enfin.

'GO, SONG, WITH THE
SPEED OF WINGS...'

Go, song, with the speed of wings,
Go, welcome her, and tell her true
That to my faithful heart she brings
An illumination new.

Tell her a blessed light dispels
All the shadow side of love:
Jealousy, distrust and fear,
And the noon sun shines above!

Silent and afraid so long,
Now do you hear it? Gaiety
Has filled the heaven with its song,
An eager lark in the bright sky.

Go then to her, artless rhyme,
No vain regret for what is past.
Greet her at this joyful time,
She who has returned at last.

«LE FOYER, LA LUEUR
ÉTROITE DE LA LAMPE...

Le foyer, la lueur étroite de la lampe;
La rêverie avec le doigt contre la tempe
Et les yeux se perdant parmi les yeux aimés;
L'heure du thé fumant et des livres fermés;
La douceur de sentir la fin de la soirée;
La fatigue charmante et l'attente adorée
De l'ombre nuptiale et de la douce nuit,
Oh! tout cela, mon rêve attendri le poursuit
Sans relâche, à travers toutes remises vaines,
Impatient des mois, furieux des semaines!

'THE HEARTH, THE LAMP, THE NARROW-CIRCLED LIGHT...'

The hearth, the lamp, the narrow-circled light;
The dream, with head on hand, so intimate;
Eyes gazing, lost, into beloved eyes;
The hour for steaming tea, when books are closed;
The sweetness when the evening's nearly gone;
Dear tiredness, darling expectation
Of nuptial shadows, night delectable,
Oh! in my tender dream I seek it all,
Unceasingly, through all the vain delays,
Impatient with the months, the weeks, the days!

«DONC, CE SERA PAR UN CLAIR JOUR D'ÉTÉ...»

Donc, ce sera par un clair jour d'été:
Le grand soleil, complice de ma joie,
Fera, parmi le satin et la soie,
Plus belle encor votre chère beauté;

Le ciel tout bleu, comme une haute tente,
Frissonnera somptueux à longs plis
Sur nos deux fronts heureux qu'auront pâlis
L'émotion du bonheur et l'attente;

Et quand le soir viendra, l'air sera doux
Qui se jouera, caressant, dans vos voiles,
Et les regards paisibles des étoiles
Bienveillamment souriront aux époux.

'SO SHALL A SUMMER'S DAY
MY HOPES FULFIL...'

So shall a summer's day my hopes fulfil:
The great sun, my accomplice in delight,
Shining amidst the silk and satin bright,
Shall make your loveliness more lovely still;

The sky, heraldic blue, like some vast tent,
Will quiver in its sumptuous festival
Over our two joyful brows, grown pale
With ecstasy of longing and content;

And when the evening comes, the gentle air
Will frolic with your veils, in mild caress,
And stars themselves look down, with kindliness,
Benign, untroubled, on the bridal pair.

Romances sans paroles   1874

ARIETTES OUBLIÉES

«*C'est l'extase langoureuse . . .*»

C'est l'extase langoureuse,
C'est la fatigue amoureuse,
C'est tous les frissons des bois
Parmi l'étreinte des brises,
C'est, vers les ramures grises,
Le chœur des petites voix.

Ô le frêle et frais murmure!
Cela gazouille et susurre,
Cela ressemble au cri doux
Que l'herbe agitée expire . . .
Tu dirais, sous l'eau qui vire,
Le roulis sourd des cailloux.

Cette âme qui se lamente
En cette plainte dormante,
C'est la nôtre, n'est-ce pas?
La mienne, dis, et la tienne,
Dont s'exhale l'humble antienne
Par ce tiède soir, tout bas?

FORGOTTEN ARIETTAS

''Tis ecstasy most languorous . . .'

'Tis ecstasy most languorous,
'Tis weariness most amorous,
'Tis all the forests' quivering
In the embraces of the breeze,
'Tis, in the grey boughs of the trees,
The tiny voices carolling.

Oh murmur cool and delicate!
Babble and prattle intimate,
It is like the gentle cry
That's sent up by the troubled grass . . .
The toss and turn, as currents pass,
Of boulders underneath the sea.

The soul that utters its lament
In this sleepy, still complaint
Is our own soul, is it not?
Say: it is mine, and it is thine,
That breathes out its submissive hymn
This sultry evening, gentle and remote?

«*Il pleure dans mon cœur . . .*»

Il pleut doucement sur la ville.
ARTHUR RIMBAUD

Il pleure dans mon cœur
Comme il pleut sur la ville;
Quelle est cette langueur
Qui pénètre mon cœur?

Ô bruit doux de la pluie
Par terre et sur les toits!
Pour un cœur qui s'ennuie
Ô le chant de la pluie!

Il pleure sans raison
Dans ce cœur qui s'écœure.
Quoi! nulle trahison? . . .
Ce deuil est sans raison.

C'est bien la pire peine
De ne savoir pourquoi,
Sans amour et sans haine,
Mon cœur a tant de peine!

'Tears fall in my heart . . .'

Rain falls softly on the town.
ARTHUR RIMBAUD

Tears fall in my heart
As rain falls on the town;
What weakness, what hurt
Does so enter my heart?

Oh soft sound of the rain
On the roofs, on the earth!
For a heart that knows pain
Oh the song of the rain!

Tears fall without cause
In this heart ill at ease.
No betrayal, no loss? . . .
This grief has no cause.

And it is the worst pain
That I cannot tell why,
Without love, without bane,
My heart feels such pain!

«*Le piano que baise une main frêle . . .*»

Le piano que baise une main frêle
Luit dans le soir rose et gris vaguement,
Tandis qu'avec un très léger bruit d'aile
Un air bien vieux, bien faible et bien charmant
Rôde discret, épeuré quasiment,
Par le boudoir longtemps parfumé d'Elle.

Qu'est-ce que c'est que ce berceau soudain
Qui lentement dorlote mon pauvre être?
Que voudrais-tu de moi, doux chant badin?
Qu'as-tu voulu, fin refrain incertain
Qui vas tantôt mourir vers la fenêtre
Ouverte un peu sur le petit jardin?

'*The piano kissed by a frail hand . . .*'

The piano kissed by a frail hand
Glows vaguely in the evening grey and rose,
While with a delicate and fluttering sound
An old tune, very faint, a-roaming goes,
Discreet and timorous, one might suppose,
About the room, where Her scent lingers round.

What is this unexpected lullaby
Which slowly my poor spirit doth cajole?
What would you of me, playful melody?
What did you want, vague, subtle harmony
Which in a moment shall give up its soul
By windows where the flowers bloom peacefully?

«*Ô triste, triste était mon âme . . .*»

Ô triste, triste était mon âme
À cause, à cause d'une femme.

Je ne me suis pas consolé
Bien que mon cœur s'en soit allé,

Bien que mon cœur, bien que mon âme
Eussent fui loin de cette femme.

Je ne me suis pas consolé,
Bien que mon cœur s'en soit allé.

Et mon cœur, mon cœur trop sensible
Dit à mon âme: Est-il possible,

Est-il possible, – le fût-il –
Ce fier exil, ce triste exil?

Mon âme dit à mon cœur: Sais-je
Moi-même, que nous veut ce piège

D'être présents bien qu'exilés,
Encore que loin en allés?

'Oh woeful, woeful was my soul . . .'

Oh woeful, woeful was my soul,
For a woman I was sorrowful.

I am not consoled today
Although my heart has gone away,

Although my heart, although my soul
Have fled from her, love to annul.

I am not consoled today
Although my heart has gone away.

And my heart, my heart that aches in me
Asks of my soul: Oh, can it be,

Oh, can it be, – oh, is it meant, –
This exile, this sad banishment?

My soul replies to my heart: Know I
Myself what this snare should signify

Of being present though far gone,
Proud exiles banished from their home?

«*L'ombre des arbres dans la rivière embrumée . . .*»

Le rossignol, qui du haut d'une branche se regarde dedans, croit être tombé dans la rivière. Il est au sommet d'un chêne et toutefois il a peur de se noyer.

CYRANO DE BERGERAC

L'ombre des arbres dans la rivière embrumée
    Meurt comme de la fumée,
Tandis qu'en l'air, parmi les ramures réelles,
    Se plaignent les tourterelles.

Combien, ô voyageur, ce paysage blême
    Te mira blême toi-même,
Et que tristes pleuraient dans les hautes feuillées
    Tes espérances noyées!

'The shadow of trees in the river haze . . .'

*The nightingale, sitting high up on a branch and looking at his
reflection in the river, thinks he has fallen in. He is at the top of an
oak tree, and yet he is afraid of drowning.*

CYRANO DE BERGERAC

The shadow of trees in the river haze
   Like vapour dies,
While in the air, the real boughs above,
   Complains the dove.

Oh, traveller, see in this landscape wan
   Your reflection,
See how sadly they weep in the leaves on high,
   Your hopes gone by!

AQUARELLES

Green

Voici des fruits, des fleurs, des feuilles et des branches,
Et puis voici mon cœur, qui ne bat que pour vous.
Ne le déchirez pas avec vos deux mains blanches,
Et qu'à vos yeux si beaux l'humble présent soit doux.

J'arrive tout couvert encore de rosée
Que le vent du matin vient glacer à mon front.
Souffrez que ma fatigue, à vos pieds reposée,
Rêve des chers instants qui la délasseront.

Sur votre jeune sein laissez rouler ma tête
Toute sonore encor de vos derniers baisers;
Laissez-la s'apaiser de la bonne tempête,
Et que je dorme un peu puisque vous reposez.

WATERCOLOURS

Green

Here are fruit, flowers, branches, foliage,
Here, too, my heart, which you alone command.
Oh, tear it not asunder with white hands,
But, with your fine eyes, bless my pilgrimage.

I come all covered still with morning dew,
Which passing winds have turned cold on my face.
At your feet let my tiredness rest in grace,
Dream of dear moments which will make it new.

Oh let my head lie still on your young breast.
It echoes, even now, with your last kiss.
After the sweet storm grant it peace like this,
And let me sleep a moment since you rest.

Streets (I)

Dansons la gigue !

J'aimais surtout ses jolis yeux,
Plus clairs que l'étoile des cieux,
J'aimais ses yeux malicieux.

Dansons la gigue !

Elle avait des façons vraiment
De désoler un pauvre amant,
Que c'en était vraiment charmant !

Dansons la gigue !

Mais je trouve encore meilleur
Le baiser de sa bouche en fleur,
Depuis qu'elle est morte à mon cœur.

Dansons la gigue !

Je me souviens, je me souviens
Des heures et des entretiens,
Et c'est le meilleur de mes biens.

Dansons la gigue !

SOHO

Streets (I)

Let's dance a jig!

Oh, how I loved her pretty eyes,
Brighter than the starry skies,
I loved the mischief in her eyes.

Let's dance a jig!

Certainly she had a way
Of filling lovers with dismay
That charmed them, this I have to say!

Let's dance a jig!

But better still, or so I find,
Is the kiss she's left behind
Since she's vanished from my mind.

Let's dance a jig!

I recall, oh I recall
Some moments in the carnival,
And that's what I prize most of all.

Let's dance a jig!

SOHO

A Poor Young Shepherd

J'ai peur d'un baiser
Comme d'une abeille.
Je souffre et je veille
Sans me reposer:
J'ai peur d'un baiser!

Pourtant j'aime Kate
Et ses yeux jolis.
Elle est délicate
Aux longs traits pâlis.
Oh! que j'aime Kate!

C'est Saint-Valentin!
Je dois et je n'ose
Lui dire au matin . . .
La terrible chose
Que Saint-Valentin!

Elle m'est promise,
Fort heureusement!
Mais quelle entreprise
Que d'être un amant
Près d'une promise!

J'ai peur d'un baiser
Comme d'une abeille.
Je souffre et je veille
Sans me reposer:
J'ai peur d'un baiser!

A Poor Young Shepherd

I'm afraid of a kiss
As I am of a bee.
I watch constantly:
Oh, what pain it is!
I'm afraid of a kiss!

And yet I love Kate
And her eyes so fine.
She is delicate,
And pale of mien.
Oh, how I love Kate!

It's St Valentine's Day!
I should and dare not
On that morning say . . .
Oh, the terror I've got
Of St Valentine's Day!

She is promised to me
Very happily!
But how hard to be
A lover quite free
Till she's married to me!

I'm afraid of a kiss
As I am of a bee.
I watch constantly:
Oh, what pain it is!
I'm afraid of a kiss!

Sagesse   1880

I

«Beauté des femmes, leur faiblesse,
et ces mains pâles . . .»

Beauté des femmes, leur faiblesse, et ces mains pâles
Qui font souvent le bien et peuvent tout le mal.
Et ces yeux, où plus rien ne reste d'animal
Que juste assez pour dire: «assez» aux fureurs mâles!

Et toujours, maternelle endormeuse des râles,
Même quand elle ment, cette voix! Matinal
Appel, ou chant bien doux à vêpre, ou frais signal,
Ou beau sanglot qui va mourir au pli des châles!...

Hommes durs! Vie atroce et laide d'ici-bas!
Ah! que du moins, loin des baisers et des combats,
Quelque chose demeure un peu sur la montagne,

Quelque chose du cœur enfantin et subtil,
Bonté, respect! Car qu'est-ce qui nous accompagne,
Et vraiment, quand la mort viendra, que reste-t-il?

I

'*Beauty of women, their weakness,
and those pale hands . . .*»

Beauty of women, their weakness, and those pale hands
Which often do good, and can do all ill,
And those eyes, where there is nothing animal,
Just enough to say 'enough' to man's demands!

And always, maternal soother of agonies,
Even when it lies, that voice! A matinal
Appeal, a song most mild at vespers, signal
Clear, a cry that in a mantle nobly dies! . . .

Oh, harsh mankind! Oh vile and heinous life!
Oh that at least, far from embrace or strife,
Something upon the summit may remain,

Some vestige of the childlike, subtle heart,
Kindness, respect! For what do we retain
When death comes, and with what do we depart?

«*Les faux beaux jours ont lui tout le jour,*
ma pauvre âme . . .»

Les faux beaux jours ont lui tout le jour, ma pauvre âme,
Et les voici vibrer aux cuivres du couchant.
Ferme les yeux, pauvre âme, et rentre sur-le-champ :
Une tentation des pires. Fuis l'Infâme.

Ils ont lui tout le jour en longs grêlons de flamme,
Battant toute vendange aux collines, couchant
Toute moisson de la vallée, et ravageant
Le ciel tout bleu, le ciel chanteur qui te réclame.

Ô pâlis, et va-t'en, lente et joignant les mains.
Si ces hiers allaient manger nos beaux demains ?
Si la vieille folie était encore en route ?

Ces souvenirs, va-t-il falloir les retuer ?
Un assaut furieux, le suprême sans doute !
Ô, va prier contre l'orage, va prier.

'*The false fine days have shone all day,*
my soul . . .'

The false fine days have shone all day, my soul,
They quiver in the copper setting sun.
Oh, close your eyes, my soul, at once go home:
Flee the temptation Diabolical.

They've shone all day, beating like ardent hail,
Struck every vintage on the hills, undone
Each harvest in the valley, overrun
The azure sky that calls you, lyrical.

Turn pale, and go, slowly, and joining hands.
Suppose we were by yesterdays unmanned?
Suppose old folly were still on its path?

Must memories be killed again, today?
A fierce attack, no doubt the ultimate!
Oh, pray against the tempest, go and pray.

«*Écoutez la chanson bien douce . . .*»

Écoutez la chanson bien douce
Qui ne pleure que pour vous plaire.
Elle est discrète, elle est légère:
Un frisson d'eau sur de la mousse!

La voix vous fut connue (et chère?),
Mais à présent elle est voilée
Comme une veuve désolée,
Pourtant comme elle encore fière,

Et dans les longs plis de son voile
Qui palpite aux brises d'automne,
Cache et montre au cœur qui s'étonne
La vérité comme une étoile.

Elle dit, la voix reconnue,
Que la bonté c'est notre vie,
Que de la haine et de l'envie
Rien ne reste, la mort venue.

Elle parle aussi de la gloire
D'être simple sans plus attendre,
Et de noces d'or et du tendre
Bonheur d'une paix sans victoire.

Accueillez la voix qui persiste
Dans son naïf épithalame.
Allez, rien n'est meilleur à l'âme
Que de faire une âme moins triste!

Elle est «en peine» et «de passage»,
L'âme qui souffre sans colère,
Et comme sa morale est claire! . . .
Écoutez la chanson bien sage.

'Oh listen to the song so sweet . . .'

Oh listen to the song so sweet
Which only weeps for your delight.
It is discreet, and it is light:
The shiver on moss of a rivulet!

The voice was known to you (and dear?),
But at present it is veiled
Like a widow unconsoled,
And yet it is still proud, like her.

And in the long folds of its veil
Which flutters in the autumn breeze,
It hides, and shows the heart amazed
The truth resplendent, sideral.

It says, the voice you recognize,
That kindness is our very life,
And that of envy, hate and strife
Nothing remains, when the body dies.

It also says how glorious
Are unalloyed simplicity,
And golden weddings, and the joy
Of peace where none's victorious.

Welcome the voice that's singing still
Its pure epithalamium.
A soul its finest task has done
In making souls less sorrowful!

Restless, it is, and *passing by*,
The soul that suffers without wrath;
How clearly, now, it shows the path! . . .
Oh, listen to the song so wise.

«*Les chères mains qui furent miennes . . .*»

Les chères mains qui furent miennes,
Toutes petites, toutes belles,
Après ces méprises mortelles
Et toutes ces choses païennes,

Après les rades et les grèves,
Et les pays et les provinces,
Royales mieux qu'au temps des princes,
Les chères mains m'ouvrent les rêves.

Mains en songe, mains sur mon âme,
Sais-je, moi, ce que vous daignâtes,
Parmi ces rumeurs scélérates,
Dire à cette âme qui se pâme?

Ment-elle, ma vision chaste
D'affinité spirituelle,
De complicité maternelle,
D'affection étroite et vaste?

Remords si cher, peine très bonne,
Rêves bénis, mains consacrées,
Ô ces mains, ses mains vénérées,
Faites le geste qui pardonne!

'Dear hands which used to be my own . . .'

Dear hands which used to be my own,
So very small, so beautiful,
Now all these errors pitiful
And all these pagan things are done,

After the sandy shores and sea,
The provinces and foreign climes,
More royal than in princes' times,
Dear hands, they open dreams to me.

Hands in a dream, hands on my soul,
Do I know what you deign to say
To this, my soul, that faints away
Amidst the heinous tales they tell?

Does it deceive, my vision chaste
Of spiritual affinity,
Of motherly complicity,
Affection narrow and vast?

Such dear remorse, such right anxiety,
Oh, blessed dreams, hands ever consecrate!
Those hands, her hands, oh hands I venerate:
Show by a gesture that you pardon me!

«*Et j'ai revu l'enfant unique . . .*»

Et j'ai revu l'enfant unique : il m'a semblé
Que s'ouvrait dans mon cœur la dernière blessure,
Celle dont la douleur plus exquise m'assure
D'une mort désirable en un jour consolé.

La bonne flèche aiguë et sa fraîcheur qui dure !
En ces instants choisis elles ont éveillé
Les rêves un peu lourds du scrupule ennuyé,
Et tout mon sang chrétien chanta la Chanson pure.

J'entends encor, je vois encor ! Loi du devoir
Si douce ! Enfin, je sais ce qu'est entendre et voir,
J'entends, je vois toujours ! Voix des bonnes pensées,

Innocence, avenir ! Sage et silencieux,
Que je vais vous aimer, vous un instant pressées,
Belles petites mains qui fermerez nos yeux !

'And I beheld again the only child . . .'

And I beheld again the only child: it seemed
As if the last wound opened in my heart,
The wound more exquisite, that by its hurt
Assured my longed-for death, and all redeemed.

The good sharp arrow and its lasting smart!
In those few moments they awoke the dream
Heavy with scruples and with tedium;
I sang the pure Song: Christian, sang my part.

I still hear, I still see! Oh, obligation
Most sweet! I know what sight and hearing mean,
I hear, now, see for ever! Righteous voice!

Innocence and future! Silent, wise,
How I shall love you, you a moment pressed,
Dear little hands that are to close our eyes!

II

«Ô mon Dieu, vous m'avez blessé d'amour . . .»

Ô mon Dieu, vous m'avez blessé d'amour
Et la blessure est encore vibrante,
Ô mon Dieu, vous m'avez blessé d'amour.

Ô mon Dieu, votre crainte m'a frappé
Et la brûlure est encor là qui tonne,
Ô mon Dieu, votre crainte m'a frappé.

Ô mon Dieu, j'ai connu que tout est vil
Et votre gloire en moi s'est installée,
Ô mon Dieu, j'ai connu que tout est vil.

Noyez mon âme aux flots de votre Vin,
Fondez ma vie au Pain de votre table,
Noyez mon âme aux flots de votre Vin.

Voici mon sang que je n'ai pas versé,
Voici ma chair indigne de souffrance,
Voici mon sang que je n'ai pas versé.

Voici mon front qui n'a pu que rougir,
Pour l'escabeau de vos pieds adorables,
Voici mon front qui n'a pu que rougir.

Voici mes mains qui n'ont pas travaillé,
Pour les charbons ardents et l'encens rare,
Voici mes mains qui n'ont pas travaillé.

II

'O my God, you have wounded me with love . . .'

O my God, you have wounded me with love,
The wound is there and it is throbbing still,
O my God, you have wounded me with love.

O my God, the fear of you has struck me,
The burn is there and it is thundering still,
O my God, the fear of you has struck me.

O my God, I've known that all is vile,
And your glory is installed in me,
O my God, I've known that all is vile.

Drown my soul in the flood-tide of your Wine,
Establish my life in the Bread of your table,
Drown my soul in the flood-tide of your Wine.

Here is my blood, Lord, which I have not shed,
Here is my flesh, Lord, which deserves not pain,
Here is my blood, Lord, which I have not shed.

Here is my brow, worthy alone to blush,
To be the stool of your beloved feet,
Here is my brow, worthy alone to blush.

Here are my hands, and they have laboured not,
To be the burning coals and incense rare,
Here are my hands, and they have laboured not.

Voici mon cœur qui n'a battu qu'en vain,
Pour palpiter aux ronces du Calvaire,
Voici mon cœur qui n'a battu qu'en vain.

Voici mes pieds, frivoles voyageurs,
Pour accourir au cri de votre grâce,
Voici mes pieds, frivoles voyageurs.

Voici ma voix, bruit maussade et menteur,
Pour les reproches de la Pénitence,
Voici ma voix, bruit maussade et menteur.

Voici mes yeux, luminaires d'erreur,
Pour être éteints aux pleurs de la prière,
Voici mes yeux, luminaires d'erreur.

Hélas, Vous, Dieu d'offrande et de pardon,
Quel est le puits de mon ingratitude,
Hélas, Vous, Dieu d'offrande et de pardon,

Dieu de terreur et Dieu de sainteté,
Hélas ! ce noir abîme de mon crime,
Dieu de terreur et Dieu de sainteté,

Vous, Dieu de paix, de joie et de bonheur,
Toutes mes peurs, toutes mes ignorances,
Vous, Dieu de paix, de joie et de bonheur,

Vous connaissez tout cela, tout cela,
Et que je suis plus pauvre que personne,
Vous connaissez tout cela, tout cela,

Mais ce que j'ai, mon Dieu, je vous le donne.

Here is my heart, which has beaten but in vain,
To quiver at the thorns of Calvary,
Here is my heart, which has beaten but in vain.

Here are my feet, those wayward travellers,
To hasten to you at the call of grace,
Here are my feet, those wayward travellers.

Here is my voice, a dull, deceitful sound,
For the reproaches of true Penitence,
Here is my voice, a dull, deceitful sound.

Here are my eyes, lights of my sinfulness,
To be extinguished by the tears of prayer,
Here are my eyes, lights of my sinfulness.

O God of pardon and of offering,
What is the depth of my ingratitude,
O God of pardon and of offering,

God awe-inspiring, God of holiness,
Alas, this sombre chasm of my crime,
God awe-inspiring, God of holiness,

You, God of peace, of joy and happiness,
All my alarm and all my ignorance,
You, God of peace, of joy and happiness,

You know it all, O God, you know it all,
And that I am poorer than anyone,
You know it all, O God, you know it all.

But what I have, my God, to you I give.

«*Je ne veux plus aimer que ma mère Marie . . .*»

Je ne veux plus aimer que ma mère Marie.
Tous les autres amours sont de commandement.
Nécessaires qu'ils sont, ma mère seulement
Pourra les allumer aux cœurs qui l'ont chérie.

C'est pour Elle qu'il faut chérir mes ennemis,
C'est par Elle que j'ai voué ce sacrifice,
Et la douceur de cœur et le zèle au service,
Comme je la priais, Elle les a permis.

Et comme j'étais faible et bien méchant encore,
Aux mains lâches, les yeux éblouis des chemins,
Elle baissa mes yeux et me joignit les mains,
Et m'enseigna les mots par lesquels on adore.

C'est par Elle que j'ai voulu de ces chagrins,
C'est par Elle que j'ai mon cœur dans les Cinq Plaies,
Et tous ces bons efforts vers les croix et les claies,
Comme je l'invoquais, Elle en ceignit mes reins.

Je ne veux plus penser qu'à ma mère Marie,
Siège de la Sagesse et source des pardons,
Mère de France aussi, de qui nous attendons
Inébranlablement l'honneur de la patrie.

Marie Immaculée, amour essentiel,
Logique de la foi cordiale et vivace,
En vous aimant qu'est-il de bon que je ne fasse,
En vous aimant du seul amour, Porte du ciel?

'My mother Mary shall be all I love . . .'

My mother Mary shall be all I love.
All other loves I have at Her command.
By Her alone the flames of light are fanned,
Essential in the hearts which loving prove.

It is for Her I cherish all my foes,
To Her this sacrifice I consecrate;
And gentleness, and zeal to dedicate,
Because I asked her, She has granted those.

And as I sinned, in weakness, as before,
With timid hands, eyes dazzled by the way,
She closed my hands, and taught me how to pray,
And found the words with which I should adore.

It is for Her I wanted to know grief,
For Her my heart lies in the Wounds divine,
And when I prayed that burdens should be mine,
She girt my loins with them, for my belief.

My mother Mary shall be all to me,
The Seat of Wisdom and the source of grace,
Mother of France, who looks with smiling face
Upon our honour for eternity.

Mary Immaculate, love vital proven,
Where piety profound must have its home,
In loving you what virtues may not come,
In loving you alone, the Gate of Heaven?

«Mon Dieu m'a dit: – Mon fils, il faut m'aimer . . .»

I

Mon Dieu m'a dit: – Mon fils, il faut m'aimer. Tu vois
Mon flanc percé, mon cœur qui rayonne et qui saigne,
Et mes pieds offensés que Madeleine baigne
De larmes, et mes bras douloureux sous le poids

De tes péchés, et mes mains! Et tu vois la croix,
Tu vois les clous, le fiel, l'éponge, et tout t'enseigne
A n'aimer, en ce monde amer où la chair règne,
Que ma Chair et mon Sang, ma parole et ma voix.

Ne t'ai-je pas aimé jusqu'à la mort moi-même,
Ô mon frère en mon Père, ô mon fils en l'Esprit,
Et n'ai-je pas souffert, comme c'était écrit?

N'ai-je pas sangloté ton angoisse suprême
Et n'ai-je pas sué la sueur de tes nuits,
Lamentable ami qui me cherches où je suis?

II

J'ai répondu: – Seigneur, vous avez dit mon âme.
C'est vrai que je vous cherche et ne vous trouve pas.
Mais vous aimer! Voyez comme je suis en bas,
Vous dont l'amour toujours monte comme la flamme.

Vous, la source de paix que toute soif réclame,
Hélas! voyez un peu tous mes tristes combats!
Oserai-je adorer la trace de vos pas,
Sur ces genoux saignants d'un rampement infâme?

Et pourtant je vous cherche en longs tâtonnements,
Je voudrais que votre ombre au moins vêtit ma honte,
Mais vous n'avez pas d'ombre, ô vous dont l'amour monte,

'My God told me: "My son, love me . . ."'

I

My God told me: 'My son, love me. Behold
My pierced side, and my heart which bleeds and shines,
My wounded feet, which Mary Magdalen
Bathes with her tears, my aching arms which hold

Your heavy sins, my hands! Behold the Cross,
The nails and sponge and gall: they are the sign
That in this bitter world where flesh doth reign
Thou shalt love just my Flesh, Blood, word and voice.

Have I not loved thee even unto death,
Oh brother in my father, son in Ghost,
Have I not suffered, as it was decreed?

Have I not shuddered for your final breath,
Have I not sweated for your agony,
Oh pitiable friend who seeks for me?'

II

I answered: 'Lord, you speak my very soul.
Indeed I seek you and I find you not.
But love you! See how lowly is my lot,
Oh you whose love flames like an aureole.

You, source of peace which every thirst would bring,
Alas! my struggles are so pitiful!
Dare I adore your footprints wonderful
Upon these knees which bleed with grovelling?

And yet, though timorous, I seek you still,
So that your shadow clothes at least my shame,
But you no shadow know, whose love is flame,

Ô vous, fontaine calme, amère aux seuls amants
De leur damnation, ô vous toute lumière
Sauf aux yeux dont un lourd baiser tient la paupière !

III

– Il faut m'aimer ! Je suis l'universel Baiser,
Je suis cette paupière et je suis cette lèvre
Dont tu parles, ô cher malade, et cette fièvre
Qui t'agite, c'est moi toujours ! Il faut oser

M'aimer ! Oui, mon amour monte sans biaiser
Jusqu'où ne grimpe pas ton pauvre amour de chèvre,
Et t'emportera, comme un aigle vole un lièvre,
Vers des serpolets qu'un ciel cher vient arroser !

Ô ma nuit claire ! ô tes yeux dans mon clair de lune !
Ô ce lit de lumière et d'eau parmi la brune !
Toute cette innocence et tout ce reposoir !

Aime-moi ! Ces deux mots sont mes verbes suprêmes,
Car étant ton Dieu tout-puissant, je peux vouloir,
Mais je ne veux d'abord que pouvoir que tu m'aimes !

IV

– Seigneur, c'est trop ! Vraiment je n'ose. Aimer qui ? Vous ?
Oh ! non ! Je tremble et n'ose. Oh ! vous aimer je n'ose,
Je ne veux pas ! Je suis indigne. Vous, la Rose
Immense des purs vents de l'Amour, ô vous, tous

Les cœurs des saints, ô Vous qui fûtes le Jaloux
D'Israël, Vous la chaste abeille qui se pose
Sur la seule fleur d'une innocence mi-close,
Quoi, *moi, moi* pouvoir *Vous* aimer ! Êtes-vous fous,

Père, Fils, Esprit? Moi, ce pécheur-ci, ce lâche,
Ce superbe, qui fait la mal comme sa tâche
Et n'a dans tous ses sens, odorat, toucher, goût,

Calm fountain, save to those determined still
Upon their own damnation: you, all light,
Except to eyes closed by a kiss to sight!'

III

'Love me! I am the universal Kiss,
I am the lips, the eyelids and the eyes
You speak of, sufferer; the cowardice
Which troubles you is also me! Dare this:

To love me! Yes, my love soars up on high,
To heights your poor love, goat-like, cannot bear,
To take you, as an eagle steals a hare,
Towards the wild thyme bathed by a dear sky.

Oh, shining night! Your eyes in my moonlight!
Oh, bed of light and water, all twilit!
Oh, resting-place! Oh, all this innocence!

Love me! This is my message from above,
For I can *will*, in my omnipotence,
But first I only want that you *could* love.'

IV

'It is too much, Lord, and I am not brave.
Love Y o u? Oh, no! I tremble and dare not,
I will not! I'm unworthy of you yet,
Oh you, vast Rose of the pure winds of Love,

The hearts of all the Saints, oh You who were
The Jealous God of Israel, You, chaste bee
That lights upon the bud of purity,
What, *I* could love *You*? Does some madness stir

Son, Father, Spirit? I, this miscreant
Who daily sins, this coward arrogant,
Who has in all his senses, touch, taste, smell,

143

Vue, ouïe, et dans tout son être – hélas ! dans tout
Son espoir et dans tout son remords – que l'extase
D'une caresse où le seul vieil Adam s'embrase ?

V

– Il faut m'aimer. Je suis Ces Fous que tu nommais,
Je suis l'Adam nouveau qui mange le vieil homme,
Ta Rome, ton Paris, ta Sparte et ta Sodome,
Comme un pauvre rué parmi d'horribles mets.

Mon amour est le feu qui dévore à jamais
Toute chair insensée, et l'évapore comme
Un parfum, – et c'est le déluge qui consomme
En son flot tout mauvais germe que je semais,

Afin qu'un jour la Croix où je meurs fût dressée
Et que par un miracle effrayant de bonté
Je t'eusse un jour à moi, frémissant et dompté.

Aime. Sors de ta nuit. Aime. C'est ma pensée
De toute éternité, pauvre âme délaissée,
Que tu dusses m'aimer, moi seul qui suis resté !

VI

– Seigneur, j'ai peur. Mon âme en moi tressaille toute.
Je vois, je sens qu'il faut vous aimer. Mais comment
Moi, *ceci*, me ferais-je, ô Vous Dieu, votre amant,
Ô Justice que la vertu des bons redoute ?

Oui, comment ? Car voici que s'ébranle la voûte
Où mon cœur creusait son ensevelissement
Et que je sens fluer à moi le firmament,
Et je vous dis : de vous à moi quelle est la route ?

Sight, hearing, and in all his being – all
His hope, all his remorse – only the bliss
Of the old Adam, fired by a caress?'

V

'Love me. I am these Fools of whom you spake,
I'm the new Adam, I devour the old,
Sparta and Sodom, Paris, Rome: behold
Of some grim banquet, helpless, I partake.

My love is fire which burns eternally
All senseless flesh, makes it evaporate
Like perfume – it's the deluge in whose spate
Are drowned the seeds that must not multiply,

So that one day the Cross on which I die
Should rise, and, wondrous generosity,
Tremulous, tamed, you should belong to me.

Love. Leave your night. Love. My philosophy,
Poor friendless soul, for all eternity,
Has been: Love me, I only stay with thee!'

VI

'I am afraid, Lord, and my soul subdued.
I see, I feel that I must give you love,
But could *this* be your lover, God above,
Just God feared by the virtuous and the good?

How could it be? Behold it shake, the tomb
Where my own heart prepared its burial;
The firmament flows to me, I can feel:
I ask you, Lord, the path by which to come.

Tendez-moi votre main, que je puisse lever
Cette chair accroupie et cet esprit malade,
Mais recevoir jamais la céleste accolade,

Est-ce possible? Un jour, pouvoir la retrouver
Dans votre sein, sur votre cœur qui fut le nôtre,
La place où reposa la tête de l'Apôtre?

VII

– Certes, si tu le veux mériter, mon fils, oui,
Et voici. Laisse aller l'ignorance indécise
De ton cœur vers les bras ouverts de mon Église
Comme la guêpe vole au lis épanoui.

Approche-toi de mon oreille. Épanches-y
L'humiliation d'une brave franchise.
Dis-moi tout sans un mot d'orgueil ou de reprise
Et m'offre le bouquet d'un repentir choisi.

Puis franchement et simplement viens à ma table,
Et je t'y bénirai d'un repas délectable
Auquel l'ange n'aura lui-même qu'assisté,

Et tu boiras le Vin de la vigne immuable
Dont la force, dont la douceur, dont la bonté
Feront germer ton sang à l'immortalité.

*

Puis, va! Garde une foi modeste en ce mystère
D'amour par quoi je suis ta chair et ta raison,
Et surtout reviens très souvent dans ma maison,
Pour y participer au Vin qui désaltère,

Au Pain sans qui la vie est une trahison,
Pour y prier mon Père et supplier ma Mère
Qu'il te soit accordé, dans l'exil de la terre,
D'être l'agneau sans cris qui donne sa toison,

Stretch out your hand to me, that I may raise
This cowering body and this ailing soul!
But to receive your love celestial,

Can that be? To discover it, one day,
Upon your heart which was our own: your breast,
The place where the Apostle's head found rest?'

VII

'Yes, that can be, my son, if you would earn
My love. Your heart, uncertain of its place,
And ignorant, must seek the wide embrace
Of my own Church, as bees seek flowers in bloom.

Come closer to me. Pour into my ear
Humiliation and brave honesty.
No pride and no denial. Confess to me.
Choose to repent: an offering most dear.

Then frankly, simply, at my Table sit,
And I shall bless thee with food exquisite
Which angels shall not taste, but only see,

And thou shalt know the vineyard consecrate,
The Wine whose strength and sweetness heavenly
Will make your blood burgeon immortally.

*

Then go! Humbly believe this mystery
Of love by which I am thy flesh, thy soul,
And come back to me often, filial,
To taste the Wine which thirst doth satisfy,

The Bread without which life is a betrayal,
And there my Father and my Mother pray
That thou, in exile temporal, may be
The lamb without a cry that gives its wool,

D'être l'enfant vêtu de lin et d'innocence,
D'oublier ton pauvre amour-propre et ton essence,
Enfin, de devenir un peu semblable à moi

Qui fus, durant les jours d'Hérode et de Pilate
Et de Judas et de Pierre, pareil à toi
Pour souffrir et mourir d'une mort scélérate !

*

Et pour récompenser ton zèle en ces devoirs
Si doux qu'ils sont encor d'ineffables délices,
Je te ferai goûter sur terre mes prémices,
La paix du cœur, l'amour d'être pauvre, et mes soirs

Mystiques, quand l'esprit s'ouvre aux calmes espoirs
Et croit boire, suivant ma promesse, au Calice
Éternel, et qu'au ciel pieux la lune glisse,
Et que sonnent les angélus roses et noirs,

En attendant l'assomption dans ma lumière,
L'éveil sans fin dans ma charité coutumière,
La musique de mes louanges à jamais,

Et l'extase perpetuelle et la science,
Et d'être en moi parmi l'aimable irradiance
De tes souffrances, enfin miennes, que j'aimais !

VIII

– Ah ! Seigneur, qu'ai-je ? Hélas ! me voici tout en larmes
D'une joie extraordinaire ! votre voix
Me fait comme du bien et du mal à la fois,
Et le mal et le bien, tout a les mêmes charmes.

The child in linen clad and innocence,
Forgetting thy poor self, thy arrogance,
And, finally, to be like unto me

Who, in the days when Herod lived on earth,
Judas, Peter and Pilate, was like thee
To suffer and to die a villain's death!

*

And to reward thy zeal in duties done
So sweet that they are pleasures infinite,
Thou shalt on earth taste heavenly delight:
Peace, love of poverty, the benison

Of evenings of calm aspiration,
When the soul tastes the Cup I promised it,
The Cup eternal, and the pious night
Is moonlit, and the Angelus rings on,

Awaiting thy assumption in my light,
And, in my charity, life infinite,
And my eternal praises sung above,

Lasting delight, the end of ignorance,
And being with me in the radiance
Of all thy pain – now mine – which earned my love!'

VIII

'What ails me, Lord? See: tears run down my face
With joy extraordinary, and your voice
Fills me, it seems, with sorrow and with bliss,
And bliss and sorrow likewise have their grace.

Je ris, je pleure, et c'est comme un appel aux armes
D'un clairon pour des champs de bataille où je vois
Des anges bleus et blancs portés sur des pavois,
Et ce clairon m'enlève en de fières alarmes.

J'ai l'extase et j'ai la terreur d'être choisi.
Je suis indigne, mais je sais votre clémence.
Ah ! quel effort, mais quelle ardeur ! Et me voici

Plein d'une humble prière, encor qu'un trouble immense
Brouille l'espoir que votre voix me révéla,
Et j'aspire en tremblant.

IX

— Pauvre âme, c'est cela !

I laugh, I weep, as if a trumpet cries
To arms, to battles and to victories,
Where angels, blue and white, on pavises
Are borne, and, eager, proud, I find my place.

I feel the terror and the ecstasy
Of being chosen. I deserve it not
But, God almighty, know your clemency.

Full of a humble prayer, I fight, devout,
A trouble vast confounds your hope for me,
Trembling, I wait . . .'

IX

      . . . 'Poor soul, thy ecstasy!'

III

«*Je suis venu, calme orphelin . . .*»

Gaspard Hauser★ *chante:*

Je suis venu, calme orphelin,
Riche des mes seuls yeux tranquilles,
Vers les hommes des grandes villes:
Ils ne m'ont pas trouvé malin.

A vingt ans un trouble nouveau
Sous le nom d'amoureuses flammes
M'a fait trouver belles les femmes:
Elles ne m'ont pas trouvé beau.

Bien que sans patrie et sans roi
Et très brave ne l'étant guère,
J'ai voulu mourir à la guerre:
La mort n'a pas voulu de moi.

Suis-je né trop tôt ou trop tard?
Qu'est-ce que je fais en ce monde?
Ô vous tous, ma peine est profonde;
Priez pour le pauvre Gaspard!

★ Gaspard Hauser was a youth of fifteen or sixteen when, in 1828, he had
been discovered wandering in the streets of Nuremburg. He had known
nothing of his origins; doctors said that he seemed to have been imprisoned
throughout his childhood, and to have been kept in a state which bordered

III

'I came, serene and fatherless . . .'

Gaspard Hauser* sings:

I came, serene and fatherless,
My peaceful eyes my whole estate,
To those who lived in cities great:
They found me unmalicious.

At twenty, an emotion new –
The flame of love, I know full well –
Made me find women beautiful:
They did not find me handsome too.

I had no country and no king,
I was not brave as warriors are,
I wanted still to die in war:
Death would not take my offering.

Why do I live? I cannot see.
Oh, was I born too soon, too late?
Oh, all of you, my grief is great:
Poor Gaspard: pray you, pray for me.

on imbecility. He was adopted and cared for, but it soon became evident
that he had some mysterious enemy. After two attempts at suicide, he was
murdered in 1833. His epitaph ran: '*Hic jacet Casparus Hauser, aenigma sui
temporis. Ignota nativitas, occulta mors.*'

«*Un grand sommeil noir . . .*»

Un grand sommeil noir
Tombe sur ma vie:
Dormez, tout espoir,
Dormez, toute envie!

Je ne vois plus rien,
Je perds la mémoire
Du mal et du bien . . .
Ô la triste histoire!

Je suis un berceau
Qu'une main balance
Au creux d'un caveau:
Silence, silence!

'*A great black sleep . . .*'

A great black sleep
Falls on me now:
Sleep, every hope,
Sleep, every vow!

I see no more,
I can't recall
Evil or good . . .
Oh, sorry tale!

A cradle I,
Rocked by a hand
Deep in a vault:
No sound, no sound!

«*Le ciel est, par-dessus le toit . . .*»

Le ciel est, par-dessus le toit,
   Si bleu, si calme !
Un arbre, par-dessus le toit,
   Berce sa palme.

La cloche dans le ciel qu'on voit
   Doucement tinte.
Un oiseau sur l'arbre qu'on voit
   Chante sa plainte.

Mon Dieu, mon Dieu, la vie est là,
   Simple et tranquille,
Cette paisible rumeur-là
   Vient de la ville.

– Qu'as-tu fait, ô toi que voilà
   Pleurant sans cesse,
Dis, qu'as-tu fait, toi que voilà,
   De ta jeunesse?

'The sky is high above the roof . . .'

The sky is high above the roof:
  So blue, so calm!
A tree which grows above the roof
  Rocks its palm.

The bell, in the blue sky I see,
  Gently rings.
A bird upon the tree I see
  Sadly sings.

My God, my God, the world is near,
  And life goes on.
That peaceful murmur that I hear
  Comes from the town.

– Where have they gone, oh you I see
  In constant tears,
Where have they gone, oh answer me,
  Your early years?

«Je ne sais pourquoi . . .»

Je ne sais pourquoi
Mon esprit amer
D'une aile inquiète et folle vole sur la mer.
Tout ce qui m'est cher,
D'une aile d'effroi
Mon amour le couve au ras des flots. Pourquoi, pourquoi?

Mouette à l'essor mélancolique,
Elle suit la vague, ma pensée,
A tous les vents du ciel balancée
Et biaisant quand la marée oblique,
Mouette à l'essor mélancolique.

Ivre de soleil
Et de liberté,
Un instinct la guide à travers cette immensité.
La brise d'été
Sur le flot vermeil
Doucement la porte en un tiède demi-sommeil.

Parfois si tristement elle crie
Qu'elle alarme au lointain le pilote,
Puis au gré du vent se livre et flotte
Et plonge, et l'aile toute meurtrie
Revole, et puis si tristement crie!

Je ne sais pourquoi
Mon esprit amer
D'une aile inquiète et folle vole sur la mer.
Tout ce qui m'est cher,
D'une aile d'effroi
Mon amour le couve au ras des flots. Pourquoi, pourquoi?

'I know not why . . .'

I know not why
My bitter soul
With wild, unquiet wing flies o'er the sea.
All that's dear to me,
In agony
My love broods on it near the waves. Oh why, oh why?

Gull in melancholy flight,
My thought pursues the ocean,
Swinging on gust and hurricane,
And slanting as the tides invite,
Gull in melancholy flight.

With sun drunk deep,
And liberty,
An instinct guides it through immensity.
Winds summery
On the coral deep
Carry it gently in a warm half-sleep.

Sometimes so grievously it cries
That it alarms the pilot far,
Then, with the wind, soars in the air,
And plunges, bruised of wing, and through the skies
Flies on, and then so grievously it cries!

I know not why
My bitter soul
With wild, unquiet wing flies o'er the sea.
All that's dear to me,
In agony
My love broods on it near the waves. Oh why, oh why?

«*Le son du cor s'afflige vers les bois . . .*»

Le son du cor s'afflige vers les bois
D'une douleur on veut croire orpheline
Qui vient mourir au bas de la colline
Parmi la brise errant en courts abois.

L'âme du loup pleure dans cette voix
Qui monte avec le soleil qui décline
D'une agonie on veut croire câline
Et qui ravit et qui navre à la fois.

Pour faire mieux cette plainte assoupie
La neige tombe à longs traits de charpie
A travers le couchant sanguinolent,

Et l'air a l'air d'être un soupir d'automne,
Tant il fait doux par ce soir monotone
Où se dorlote un paysage lent.

'The horn among the woods makes its lament ...'

The horn among the woods makes its lament,
A sound like orphans' desolation,
Till, where the hill begins, at last it's gone:
In sudden gusts of the north wind it's spent.

The spirit of the wolf here weeps complaint,
Its burden rising as the sun sinks down,
Its agony sounds like affection,
And brings distress as well as ravishment.

Now, ministering to this drowsy plaint,
The snow falls in long bandages of lint
Across the setting sun incarnadine.

The mild air seems to be an autumn sigh
This evening when, in dull monotony,
Slowly the landscape curls in its cocoon.

«*La mer est plus belle que les cathédrales . . .*»

La mer est plus belle
Que les cathédrales,
Nourrice fidèle,
Berceuse de râles,
La mer sur qui prie
La Vierge Marie !

Elle a tous les dons
Terribles et doux.
J'entends ses pardons
Gronder ses courroux . . .
Cette immensité
N'a rien d'entêté.

Oh ! si patiente,
Même quand méchante !
Un souffle ami hante
La vague, et nous chante :
«Vous sans espérance,
Mourez sans souffrance !»

Et puis sous les cieux
Qui s'y rient plus clairs,
Elle a des airs bleus,
Roses, gris et verts . . .
Plus belle que tous,
Meilleure que nous !

'The sea's lovelier than cathedrals are . . .'

The sea's lovelier
Than cathedrals are.
Faithful abigail,
All pain it lulls.
She prays for its good,
Mary, Mother of God!

All things in it dwell,
Sweet and terrible!
Its pardon I hear
Scold its anger severe . . .
It is infinite
But not obstinate.

Oh! so merciful
Even when it is cruel!
A kindly breeze haunts
The ocean, and chants:
'Your hope has all gone,
Die without pain!'

And under the sky,
In bright revelry,
It looks ultramarine,
Roseate, grey and green . . .
Oh, most beauteous!
Better than us!

«*C'est la fête du blé, c'est la fête du pain . . .*»

C'est la fête du blé, c'est la fête du pain
Aux chers lieux d'autrefois revus après ces choses !
Tout bruit, la nature et l'homme, dans un bain
De lumière si blanc que les ombres sont roses.

L'or des pailles s'effondre au vol siffleur des faux
Dont l'éclair plonge, et va luire, et se réverbère.
La plaine, tout au loin couverte de travaux,
Change de face à chaque instant, gaie et sévère.

Tout halète, tout n'est qu'effort et mouvement
Sous le soleil, tranquille auteur des moissons mûres,
Et qui travaille encore imperturbablement
A gonfler, à sucrer là-bas les grappes sures.

Travaille, vieux soleil, pour le pain et le vin,
Nourris l'homme du lait de la terre, et lui donne
L'honnête verre où rit un peu d'oubli divin.
Moissonneurs, vendangeurs là-bas ! votre heure est bonne !

Car sur la fleur des pains et sur la fleur des vins,
Fruit de la force humaine en tous lieux répartie,
Dieu moissonne, et vendange, et dispose à ses fins
La Chair et le Sang pour le calice et l'hostie !

'Behold, this festival of loaves and grain . . .'

Behold, this festival of loaves and grain
In sweet, remembered fields we celebrate!
Mankind and nature murmur in a rain
Of silver light where shade is roseate.

The golden straw gives way beneath the hiss
And glisten of the swift, reflecting scythe;
The plain reveals the work of genesis,
And changes every moment, stern and blithe.

The world is toiling, breathing heavily
Beneath the sun, who gilds the crop, serene,
And labours even now, unceasingly,
To swell and sweeten all the clusters green.

Strive on, thou ancient sun, for bread and wine,
Feed man with milk of earth, and to him give
A goblet of oblivion divine . . .
Oh! reapers, vintagers, you learn to live!

For of the flower of the bread and wine,
The fruit of human strength to furthermost
Domain, God reaps, and unto His design
Disposes Flesh and Blood as cup and host!

Jadis et Naguère   1885

SONNETS ET AUTRES VERS

Kaléidoscope

Dans une rue, au cœur d'une ville de rêve,
Ce sera comme quand on a déjà vécu:
Un instant à la fois très vague et très aigu...
Ô ce soleil parmi la brume qui se lève!

Ô ce cri sur la mer, cette voix dans les bois!
Ce sera comme quand on ignore des causes:
Un lent réveil après bien des métempsychoses:
Les choses seront plus les mêmes qu'autrefois

Dans cette rue, au cœur de la ville magique
Où des orgues moudront des gigues dans les soirs,
Où les cafés auront des chats sur les dressoirs,
Et que traverseront des bandes de musique.

Ce sera si fatal qu'on en croira mourir:
Des larmes ruisselant douces le long des joues,
Des rires sanglotés dans le fracas des roues,
Des invocations à la mort de venir,

Des mots anciens comme un bouquet de fleurs fanées!
Les bruits aigres des bals publics arriveront,
Et des veuves avec du cuivre après leur front,
Paysannes, fendront la foule des traînées

Qui flânent là, causant avec d'affreux moutards
Et des vieux sans sourcils que la dartre enfarine,
Cependant qu'à deux pas, dans des senteurs d'urine,
Quelque fête publique enverra des pétards.

SONNETS AND OTHER POEMS

Kaleidoscope

In a street, in the heart of a city in a dream,
It will be as if one had lived in earlier years:
A moment both very vague and very clear . . .
Oh, amid the rising mist that sun supreme!

Oh that cry on the sea, that voice among the trees!
It will be as if one stirred, all questioning,
After many a change of soul awakening:
And things will be more the same than formerly

In this street, in the heart of this city magical,
Where organs will grind out jigs at evening time,
Where cats will sit on the dressers in the inns,
And bands will cross the street in carnival.

It will be so fatal one will expect to die:
And the tears will stream, refreshing, down one's face,
Broken laughter will be mixed with the din of wheels,
And there will be calls upon eternity,

Withered phrases like a bouquet of faded flowers!
The cacophony of dance-halls will be heard,
And widows come with copper on their brows,
Peasants, pushing their way through the loiterers

Who linger on, talking with ragamuffins foul,
Old men without eyebrows, white with scrofula,
While, nearby, in a stench of urinals,
Crack the petards of some public festival.

Ce sera comme quand on rêve et qu'on s'éveille !
Et que l'on se rendort et que l'on rêve encor
De la même féerie et du même décor,
L'été, dans l'herbe, au bruit moiré d'un vol d'abeille.

It will be as if one dreamed, and awoke to light,
And went back to sleep again, and dreamed again
Of the same fairytale, same fairyland,
In the summer grass, while a bee's in silky flight.

Art poétique

De la musique avant toute chose,
Et pour cela préfère l'Impair
Plus vague et plus soluble dans l'air,
Sans rien en lui qui pèse ou qui pose.

Il faut aussi que tu n'ailles point
Choisir tes mots sans quelque méprise:
Rien de plus cher que la chanson grise
Où l'Indécis au Précis se joint.

C'est des beaux yeux derrière des voiles,
C'est le grand jour tremblant de midi,
C'est, par un ciel d'automne attiédi,
Le bleu fouillis des claires étoiles!

Car nous voulons la Nuance encor,
Pas la Couleur, rien que la nuance!
Oh! la nuance seule fiance
Le rêve au rêve et la flûte au cor!

Fuis du plus loin la Pointe assassine,
L'Esprit cruel et le Rire impur,
Qui font pleurer les yeux de l'Azur,
Et tout cet ail de basse cuisine!

Prends l'éloquence et tords-lui son cou!
Tu feras bien, en train d'énergie,
De rendre un peu la Rime assagie,
Si l'on n'y veille, elle ira jusqu'où?

Oh! qui dira les torts de la Rime?
Quel enfant sourd ou quel nègre fou
Nous a forgé ce bijou d'un sou
Qui sonne creux et faux sous la lime?

The Art of Poetry

Above all things be musical,
And so prefer uneven lines
Where nothing settles or confines,
Dissolving, insubstantial.

Remember also it is wrong
To choose words unambiguous.
Let Imprecise melt in Precise:
Nothing more dear than silver song.

It is fine eyes behind a veil,
The broad and trembling light of noon,
The blue confusion of bright moon
On afternoons autumnal, cool!

For we must have the Nuance still,
Not Colour, only the nuance!
For shades alone can affiance
Dream unto dream, or flute to viol!

Escape from lethal Quiddity,
From cruel Wit, and Laughter cheap:
It makes the eyes of Heaven weep,
That garlic from the scullery!

Take eloquence and strangle it!
While you're about it, you'll do well
To make the Rhyme more sensible,
If you don't watch, where will she flit?

Oh who can tell the wrongs of Rhyme?
What deafened child, savage insane
Has trumped up this unprecious stone
Which rings false to the file each time?

De la musique encore et toujours !
Que ton vers soit la chose envolée
Qu'on sent qui fuit d'une âme en allée
Vers d'autres cieux à d'autres amours.

Que ton vers soit la bonne aventure
Éparse au vent crispé du matin
Qui va fleurant la menthe et le thym . . .
Et tout le reste est littérature.

Music again and evermore!
May your verse be the thing that's flown,
Escaping from a spirit gone
To loves and skies unknown before.

May your verse be the luck in store
That's scattered on the morning wind
Which smells of mint and thyme it finds . . .
And all the rest is literature.

Allégorie

Despotique, pesant, incolore, l'Été,
Comme un roi fainéant présidant un supplice,
S'étire par l'ardeur blanche du ciel complice
Et bâille. L'homme dort loin du travail quitté.

L'alouette au matin, lasse, n'a pas chanté,
Pas un nuage, pas un souffle, rien qui plisse
Ou ride cet azur implacablement lisse
Où le silence bout dans l'immobilité.

L'âpre engourdissement a gagné les cigales
Et sur leur lit étroit de pierres inégales
Les ruisseaux à moitié taris ne sautent plus.

Une rotation incessante de moires
Lumineuses étend ses flux et ses reflux . . .
Des guêpes, çà et là, volent, jaunes et noires.

Allegory

Summer, despotic, sluggish, colourless,
Like a king idly watching an execution,
Stretches under the torrid sky, its minion,
And yawns. The labourer yields to drowsiness.

The lark did not sing today, for weariness,
Not a cloud, not a breath, disturbs the halcyon
And implacably smooth sky, the pavilion
Where silence broods sullen and motionless.

The bitter torpor has reached the cicadas.
On their stony bed, narrow and devious,
The rivers are half dried-up and rush no more.

Luminous waves, unceasingly unrolled,
Spread out their ebb and flow along the shore . . .
Here and there, the wasps fly, black and gold.

A LA MANIÈRE DE PLUSIEURS

La Princesse Bérénice

Sa tête fine dans sa main toute petite,
Elle écoute le chant des cascades lointaines,
Et, dans la plainte langoureuse des fontaines,
Perçoit comme un écho béni du nom de Tite.

Elle a fermé ses yeux divins de clématite
Pour bien leur peindre, au cœur des batailles hautaines
Son doux héros, le mieux aimant des capitaines,
Et, Juive, elle se sent au pouvoir d'Aphrodite.

Alors un grand souci la prend d'être amoureuse,
Car dans Rome une loi bannit, barbare, affreuse,
Du trône impérial toute femme étrangère.

Et sous le noir chagrin dont sanglote son âme,
Entre les bras de sa servante la plus chère,
La reine, hélas ! défaille et tendrement se pâme.

IN THE STYLE OF
VARIOUS POETS

Princess Berenice

Her fine head on her small hand lies at rest;
She listens to the song of far cascades,
And, in the fountains' drowsy serenades,
She hears the name of Titus, echo blessed.

She's closed her heavenly eyes of clematis
To picture, in the heart of the great fight,
Her gentle hero, captain of delight,
And, Jewess, in the power of Venus is.

Then she is frightened to be amorous,
For Roman law, dreadful and barbarous,
Bans foreign women from the imperial throne.

And, as her soul sobs in black misery,
Into the arms of her dear minion
The queen tenderly falters and faints away.

Langueur

Je suis l'Empire à la fin de la décadence,
Qui regarde passer les grands Barbares blancs
En composant des acrostiches indolents
D'un style d'or où la langueur du soleil danse.

L'âme seulette a mal au cœur d'un ennui dense,
Là-bas on dit qu'il est de longs combats sanglants.
Ô n'y pouvoir, étant si faible aux vœux si lents,
Ô n'y vouloir fleurir un peu cette existence!

Ô n'y vouloir, ô n'y pouvoir mourir un peu!
Ah! tout est bu! Bathylle, as-tu fini de rire?
Ah! tout est bu, tout est mangé! plus rien à dire!

Seul, un poème un peu niais qu'on jette au feu,
Seul, un esclave un peu coureur qui vous néglige,
Seul, un ennui d'on ne sait quoi qui vous afflige!

Languor

I am the Empire late in the decadence,
Watching the white Barbarians as they pass,
Making acrostics up in my idleness
In a golden style of sunlit indolence.

Only the soul wilts with tedium intense.
Battles, they say, are raging, merciless.
Oh, not to want, in weakness and feebleness,
Oh, not to hope to enlarge experience!

Oh, not to want, to be able to try to die!
Ah! All is drunk! Bathyllus, you laugh away!
Ah! All is drunk, all eaten! There's naught to say!

Only a poem to burn – it was written stupidly;
Only a roving slave, who pays no attention,
Only a causeless boredom, grievous affliction!

Amour 1888

UN VEUF PARLE

Je vois un groupe sur la mer.
Quelle mer? Celle de mes larmes!
Mes yeux mouillés du vent amer
Dans cette nuit d'ombre et d'alarmes
Sont deux étoiles sur la mer.

C'est une toute jeune femme
Et son enfant déjà tout grand
Dans une barque où nul ne rame,
Sans mât ni voile, en plein courant . . .
Un jeune garçon, une femme!

En plein courant dans l'ouragan!
L'enfant se cramponne à sa mère
Qui ne sait plus où, non plus qu'en . . .
Ni plus rien, et qui, folle, espère
En le courant, en l'ouragan.

Espérez en Dieu, pauvre folle,
Crois en notre Père, petit.
La tempête qui vous désole,
Mon cœur de là-haut vous prédit
Qu'elle va cesser, petit, folle!

Et paix au groupe sur la mer,
Sur cette mer de bonnes larmes!
Mes yeux joyeux dans le ciel clair,
Par cette nuit sans plus d'alarmes,
Sont deux bons anges sur la mer.

A WIDOWER SPEAKS

I see a vision on the sea.
Which sea? The ocean of my tears.
My eyes are wet, for bitterly
It blows on this dark night of fears,
My eyes are two stars on the sea.

A woman, youthful still, appears,
Beside her child, already grown,
In a small boat which no one steers;
No mast, no sail, by currents thrown . . .
A woman, a young boy, appear!

By current thrown, by tempest tossed!
The young boy to his mother clings,
She knows not where or what, is lost . . .
Knows nothing, hopes in anything,
Hopes in the tide, in tempest tossed.

Hope thou in God, poor foolish soul,
Believe thou in our Father, child.
The storms that rage, the seas that roll,
My heart foretells they will be stilled,
They will be calmed, child, foolish soul!

Peace to the vision on the sea,
Upon the ocean of sweet tears!
My joyful eyes in the clear sky,
Upon this night with no more fears,
Are two good angels on the sea.

LUCIEN LÉTINOIS

«Mon fils est mort. J'adore, ô mon Dieu, votre loi . . .»

Mon fils est mort. J'adore, ô mon Dieu, votre loi.
Je vous offre les pleurs d'un cœur presque parjure;
Vous châtiez bien fort et parferez la foi
Qu'alanguissait l'amour pour une créature.

Vous châtiez bien fort. Mon fils est mort, hélas!
Vous me l'aviez donné, voici que votre droite
Me le reprend à l'heure où mes pauvres pieds las
Réclamaient ce cher guide en cette route étroite.

Vous me l'aviez donné, vous me le reprenez:
Gloire à vous! J'oubliais beaucoup trop votre gloire
Dans la langueur d'aimer mieux les trésors donnés
Que le Munificent de toute cette histoire.

Vous me l'aviez donné, je vous le rends très pur,
Tout pétri de vertu, d'amour et de simplesse.
C'est pourquoi, pardonnez, Terrible, à celui sur
Le cœur de qui, Dieu fort, sévit cette faiblesse.

Et laissez-moi pleurer et faites-moi bénir
L'élu dont vous voudrez certes que la prière
Rapproche un peu l'instant si bon de revenir
A lui dans Vous, Jésus, après ma mort dernière.

LUCIEN LÉTINOIS

'My son is dead. O Lord my God, I worship your decree . . .'

My son is dead. O Lord my God, I worship your decree.
I offer you the sorrow of a heart almost forsworn.
You chastise bitterly to prove the worth of piety
Weakened by love of humankind, of one who was earth-born.

You chastise very bitterly. My son is dead, alas!
You gave him to me. Now behold your right hand in its wrath
Takes him away from me when in my grief and weariness
I needed this beloved guide along the narrow path.

You gave him unto me, and now you take him back from me:
To you be glory! I forgot your glory much too soon,
For I, in weakness, loved the sign of generosity,
Not the Munificent himself from whom the gift had come.

You gave him unto me, immaculate is him I give,
Compact of virtue, lovingkindness, and simplicity.
And so, O God of vengeance, God most terrible, forgive
The man you punished rigorously for this frailty.

And let me shed my tears, Almighty God, and make me bless
Your own elect, whose prayer, you must desire most certainly,
Brings ever nearer my approaching time of happiness,
When I find him in you, O Jesus Christ, eternally.

«Ô l'odieuse obscurité . . .»

Ô l'odieuse obscurité
Du jour le plus gai de l'année
Dans la monstrueuse cité
Où se fit notre destinée !

Au lieu du bonheur attendu,
Quel deuil profond, quelles ténèbres !
J'en étais comme un mort, et tu
Flottais en des pensers funèbres.

La nuit croissait avec le jour
Sur notre vitre et sur notre âme,
Tel un pur, un sublime amour
Qu'eût étreint la luxure infâme;

Et l'affreux brouillard refluait
Jusqu'en la chambre où la bougie
Semblait un reproche muet
Pour quelque lendemain d'orgie.

Un remords de péché mortel
Serrait notre cœur solitaire . . .
Puis notre désespoir fut tel
Que nous oubliâmes la terre,

Et que, pensant au seul Jésus
Né rien que pour nous ce jour même,
Notre foi prenant le dessus
Nous éclaira du jour suprême.

– Bonne tristesse qu'aima Dieu !
Brume dont se voilait la Grâce,
Crainte que l'éclat de son feu
Ne fatiguât notre âme lasse.

'Oh odious obscurity . . .'

Oh odious obscurity
Of the year's most cheerful day!
City of immensity
Where we met our destiny!

Instead of the expected joy,
Deep mourning and oppressive gloom!
It was like a death to me,
And you with morbid thoughts were dumb.

The night grew longer with the day,
Our window and our soul o'ercast,
As if great love without alloy
Had been embraced by vicious lust;

And the dreadful fog flowed on
Into the room: the candle bright
Seemed a dumb accusation
After some orgiastic night.

Then remorse for mortal sin
Gripped our solitary hearts . . .
And, such our desperation,
That in it we forgot the earth,

And, thinking only of Our Lord,
Born on this day for us alone,
Our faith new comfort did afford,
And with a light sublime it shone.

Good affliction, dear to God!
Mist by which His grace was veiled
So that its brilliance was subdued
And did not tire our weary soul.

Délicates attentions
D'une Providence attendrie ! . . .
Ô parfois encore soyons
Ainsi tristes, âme chérie !

Oh, thoughtfulness most delicate
Of a tender Providence! . . .
May despair again await
Our souls, to know such recompense!

«*Cette adoption de toi pour mon enfant . . .*»

Cette adoption de toi pour mon enfant
Puisque l'on m'avait volé mon fils réel,
Elle n'était pas dans les conseils du ciel,
Je me le suis dit, en pleurant, bien souvent;

Je me le suis dit toujours devant ta tombe
Noire de fusains, blanche de marguerites;
Elle fut sans doute un de ces démérites
Cause de ces maux où voici que je tombe.

Ce fut, je le crains, un faux raisonnement.
A bien réfléchir, je n'avais pas le droit,
Pour me consoler dans mon chemin étroit,
De te choisir, même ô si naïvement,

Même ô pour ce plan d'humble vertu cachée:
Quelques champs autour d'une maison sans faste
Que connaît le pauvre, et sur un bonheur chaste
La grâce de Dieu complaisamment penchée!

Fallait te laisser, pauvre et gai, dans ton nid,
Ne pas te mêler à mes jeux orageux,
Et souffrir l'exil en proscrit courageux,
L'exil loin du fils né d'un amour bénit.

Il me reviendrait, le fils des justes noces,
A l'époque d'être au moment d'être un homme,
Quand il comprendrait, quand il sentirait comme
Son père endura de sottises féroces!

Cette adoption fut le fruit défendu;
J'aurais dû passer dans l'odeur et le frais
De l'arbre et du fruit sans m'arrêter auprès.
Le ciel m'a puni . . . J'aurais dû, j'aurais dû!

'This adoption of you as my son . . .'

This adoption of you as my son,
Since they had taken my real child from me,
Was not an act which heaven smiled to see,
I've told myself, so often, since you've gone;

I told myself, again, beside your tomb
Sombre with spindle-trees, with daisies white;
In this again I did not act aright,
I was unworthy, I invited doom.

It was, I fear, an unfair argument.
I know now that it was not right of me
To seek for comfort in my calvary,
By choosing you, even though innocent,

Oh, even for our virtuous solitude:
A few fields round an unpretentious house
Known to the poor – unsullied happiness
Watched over by the kindly grace of God!

I should have left you, gay, in your poor nest,
Not drawn you into my wild firmament,
And, brave in exile, suffered banishment,
Far from the son once born of marriage blessed.

He would come back to me, my lawful child,
The very moment his real life began,
And he would understand, feel, as a man,
The savage way his father was reviled!

It was forbidden fruit, adoption!
I should have passed the freshness and the scent
Of tree and fruit, and with them been content.
And now . . . I should have known, I should have known!

«*Âme, te souvient-il, au fond du paradis . . .*»

Âme, te souvient-il, au fond du paradis,
De la gare d'Auteuil et des trains de jadis
T'amenant chaque jour, venus de La Chapelle?
Jadis déjà! Combien pourtant je me rappelle
Mes stations au bas du rapide escalier
Dans l'attente de toi, sans pouvoir oublier
Ta grâce en descendant les marches, mince et leste
Comme un ange le long de l'échelle céleste,
Ton sourire amical ensemble et filial,
Ton serrement de main cordial et loyal,
Ni tes yeux d'innocent, doux mais vifs, clairs et sombres,
Qui m'allaient droit au cœur et pénétraient mes ombres.
Après les premiers mots de bonjour et d'accueil,
Mon vieux bras dans le tien, nous quittions cet Auteuil
Et, sous les arbres pleins d'une gente musique,
Notre entretien était souvent métaphysique.
Ô tes forts arguments, ta foi du charbonnier!
Non sans quelque tendance, ô si franche! à nier,
Mais si vite quittée au premier pas du doute!
Et puis nous rentrions, plus que lents, par la route
Un peu des écoliers, chez moi, chez nous plutôt,
Y déjeuner de rien, fumailler vite et tôt,
Et dépêcher longtemps une vague besogne.

Mon pauvre enfant, ta voix dans le Bois de Boulogne!

'Soul, do you remember, deep in paradise sublime...'

Soul, do you remember, deep in paradise sublime,
The railway station at Auteuil, the trains of former times
That brought you to me every day, coming from La Chapelle?
Already former times! And yet how clearly I recall
How I would stand there, waiting, at the foot of the steep stairs,
Waiting for you to come; and, even now, I am aware
Of your uncommon grace as you ran down the steps, agile,
Slim, like an angel gliding down the stairs celestial.
You smiled at me – a smile at once friendly and filial –
And shook my hand: your grasp was both faithful and cordial.
Your eyes were innocent, gentle but bright, both dark and light,
They went straight to my heart, straight through my night,
After the first good mornings, the first greetings, had been said,
My old arm linked in yours, we left Auteuil, and walked ahead,
Beneath the green trees which sent down their music lyrical.
Our conversation was often metaphysical.
Oh, your implicit faith, and your determined argument!
Though you did have a tendency – so frank! – towards dissent,
But you changed your mind so quickly, at the slightest doubt!
And then we made our way back home, taking a roundabout
Path, walking very slowly, to my house, or, rather, ours,
To snatch a lunch and puff away at our pipes for an hour,
And linger over some vague task, left always unfulfilled.

Oh, your voice in the Bois de Boulogne! Oh, my beloved
    child!

«*Si tu ne mourus pas entre mes bras . . .*»

Si tu ne mourus pas entre mes bras,
Ce fut tout comme, et de ton agonie,
J'en vis assez, ô détresse infinie!
Tu délirais, plus pâle que tes draps;

Tu me tenais, d'une voix trop lucide,
Des propos doux et fous, «que j'étais mort,
Que c'était triste,» et tu serrais très fort
Ma main tremblante, et regardais à vide;

Je me tournais, n'en pouvant plus de pleurs,
Mais ta fièvre voulait suivre son thème,
Tu m'appelais par mon nom de baptême,
Puis ce fut tout, ô douleur des douleurs!

J'eusse en effet dû mourir à ta place,
Toi debout, là, présidant nos adieux!...
Je dis cela faute de dire mieux.
Et pardonnez, Dieu juste, à mon audace.

'*Although you did not die in my embrace . . .*'

Although you did not die in my embrace,
It was as if you did; your agony,
Sorrow immense, was my own calvary.
Your sheets were not as pallid as your face;

You spoke to me, clear but delirious,
And told me sweet, wild things, 'that I was dead,
That it was sad,' and, to be comforted,
Held fast my hand, and gazed on emptiness.

I trembled, turned away to hide my grief,
But in your fevered way you still talked on,
Talked to me, called me by my Christian name,
Then that was all, oh pain beyond belief!

I should have found my own eternity,
With you standing beside me in farewell ! . . .
I tell you now, there's nothing else to tell.
And, just God, pardon my audacity.

Parallèlement   1889

LES AMIES

Sur le balcon

Toutes deux regardaient s'enfuir les hirondelles:
L'une pâle aux cheveux de jais, et l'autre blonde
Et rose, et leurs peignoirs légers de vieille blonde
Vaguement serpentaient, nuages, autour d'elles.

Et toutes deux, avec des langueurs d'asphodèles,
Tandis qu'au ciel montait la lune molle et ronde,
Savouraient à longs traits l'émotion profonde
Du soir et le bonheur triste des cœurs fidèles.

Telles, leurs bras pressant, moites, leurs tailles souples,
Couple étrange qui prend pitié des autres couples,
Telles, sur le balcon, rêvaient les jeunes femmes.

Derrière elles, au fond du retrait riche et sombre,
Emphatique comme un trône de mélodrames
Et plein d'odeurs, le Lit, défait, s'ouvrait dans l'ombre.

LESBIANS

On the Balcony

They looked on as the swallows flew away:
One sallow, with jet hair, the other blonde
And pink-cheeked, and their light wraps of old blonde
Lay on them, cloud-like, in vague disarray.

And both of them, languid as asphodels,
While, soft and round, the moon rose in the sky,
Savoured at length the deep serenity
Of evening, the sad joy of love reciprocal.

So, damp arms round each other's yielding waists,
Strange pair who pitied those in men's embrace,
So, on the balcony, the girls dreamed on.

Behind them, in the rich and private room,
Emphatic like a melodrama throne,
The Bed, unmade, and fragrant, in the gloom.

RÉVÉRENCE PARLER

Impression fausse

Dame souris trotte,
Noire dans le gris du soir,
Dame souris trotte
Grise dans le noir.

On sonne la cloche,
Dormez, les bons prisonniers,
On sonne la cloche :
Faut que vous dormiez.

Pas de mauvais rêve,
Ne pensez qu'à vos amours.
Pas de mauvais rêve :
Les belles toujours !

Le grand clair de lune !
On ronfle ferme à côté.
Le grand clair de lune
En réalité !

Un nuage passe,
Il fait noir comme en un four.
Un nuage passe.
Tiens, le petit jour !

Dame souris trotte,
Rose dans les rayons bleus.
Dame souris trotte :
Debout, paresseux !

WITH RESPECT

False Impression

Madam mouse runs about,
She is black in the grey half-light,
Madam mouse runs about
Grey in black of night.

Bells ring out, day is done,
Sleep you well, good prisoners!
Bells ring out, day is done:
No prisoner now stirs.

Evil dreams disturb you not,
Think only of your sweethearts here.
Evil dreams disturb you not:
Oh mistresses most dear!

Moonlight bright, oh moonlight bright!
They're snoring hard beside me now.
Moonlight bright, oh moonlight bright
It is undoubtedly!

A sombre cloud drifts overhead,
It is dark as a furnace here.
A sombre cloud drifts overhead.
Oh, let the day appear!

Madam mouse runs about,
She is pink as the blue light comes.
Madam mouse runs about:
Now get up, lazybones!

MAINS

Ce ne sont pas des mains d'altesse,
De beau prélat quelque peu saint,
Pourtant une délicatesse
Y laisse son galbe succinct.

Ce ne sont pas des mains d'artiste,
De poète, proprement dit,
Mais quelque chose comme triste
En fait comme un groupe en petit;

Car les mains ont leur caractère,
C'est tout un monde en mouvement
Où la pouce et l'auriculaire
Donnent les pôles de l'aimant.

Les météores de la tête
Comme les tempêtes du cœur,
Tout s'y répète et s'y reflète
Par un don logique et vainqueur.

Ce ne sont pas non plus les palmes
D'un rural ou d'un faubourien;
Encor leurs grandes lignes calmes
Disent: «Travail qui ne doit rien.»

Elles sont maigres, longues, grises,
Phalange large, ongle carré.
Tels en ont aux vitraux d'églises
Les saints sous le rinceau doré,

Ou tels quelques vieux militaires
Déshabitués des combats
Se rappellent leurs longues guerres
Qu'ils narrent entre haut et bas.

HANDS

These are not a prince's hands,
The hands of a fine prelate, quite a saint,
And yet their graceful curve commands
Respect: shows delicacy and restraint.

These are not an artist's hands,
A poet's hands, the truth to tell,
But something rather sad remains
Which gives them life, like figures small;

Because hands have their character,
They are a world alive and whole
Where the thumb and little finger
Represent magnetic poles.

The solar system of the head
And the storms of heart and soul
Can all within the hand be read
By a triumph logical.

Moreover, these are not the palms
Of country or suburban man;
And yet their lines, both strong and calm,
Say: 'I owe naught to anyone.'

They are grey and sinuous,
Large of phalanx, square of nail,
Like they have in the stained glass,
The saints in golden pastoral.

Or like they have, old veterans,
Disaccustomed now to wars,
Remembering their long campaigns,
Narrating them for evermore.

Ce soir elles ont, ces mains sèches,
Sous leurs rares poils hérissés,
Des airs spécialement rêches,
Comme en proie à d'âpres pensers.

Le noir souci qui les agace,
Leur quasi-songe aigre les font
Faire une sinistre grimace
A leur façon, mains qu'elles sont.

J'ai peur à les voir sur la table,
Préméditer là, sous mes yeux,
Quelque chose de redoubtable,
D'inflexible et de furieux.

La main droite est bien à ma droite,
L'autre à ma gauche, je suis seul.
Les linges dans la chambre étroite
Prennent des aspects de linceul.

Dehors le vent hurle sans trêve,
Le soir descend insidieux . . .
Ah ! si ce sont des mains de rêve,
Tant mieux, – ou tant pis, – ou tant mieux !

This evening these dry hands possess,
Beneath their sparse and bristling hairs,
A look of special bitterness,
As if by dreadful thoughts ensnared.

The sombre terror leaves its trace:
Their disturbing reverie
Gives them a sinister grimace
That's all their own, hands that they be.

I fear to see them, on the table,
Planning there, before my eyes,
Something I fear redoubtable,
A deed both wild and merciless.

One's on my right, no question,
One's on my left, alone I brood.
The curtains in the narrow room
Assume the likeness of a shroud.

Outside the wind howls endlessly,
The evening falls in turpitude . . .
If these are hands in reverie,
All to the good, – or bad, – or good!

LAETI ET ERRABUNDI

Les courses furent intrépides
(Comme aujourd'hui le repos pèse!)
Par les steamers et les rapides.
(Que me veut cet *at home* obèse?)

Nous allions, – vous en souvient-il,
Voyageur où ça disparu? –
Filant légers dans l'air subtil,
Deux spectres joyeux, on eût cru!

Car les passions satisfaites
Insolemment outre mesure
Mettaient dans nos têtes des fêtes
Et dans nos sens, que tout rassure,

Tout, la jeunesse, l'amitié,
Et nos cœurs, ah! que dégagés
Des femmes prises en pitié
Et du dernier des préjugés,

Laissant la crainte de l'orgie
Et le scrupule au bon ermite,
Puisque quand la borne est franchie
Ponsard ne veut plus de limite.

Entre autres blâmables excès
Je crois que nous bûmes de tout,
Depuis les plus grands vins français
Jusqu'à ce faro, jusqu'au stout,

En passant par les eaux-de-vie
Qu'on cite comme redoubtables.
L'âme au septième ciel ravie,
Le corps, plus humble, sous les tables.

LAETI ET ERRABUNDI

The travels were adventurous
(How heavy lies my rest today!)
By packet-boat and by express
(Why turgid domesticity?).

We slipped away – do you recall,
O traveller lost none knows where? –
Sped through the air ethereal,
Blithe spirits in the atmosphere!

Because our passions physical,
Fulfilled to insolent excess,
Gave both our souls a festival,
Our senses, too, which all things blessed:

All things: our friendship and our youth,
Our hearts, and, oh! our hearts were freed
From women, whom we found uncouth,
And from the fear of gross misdeed.

All fear of orgies, all mistrust
We left for the ascetic good,
For once the boundary was crossed,
Ponsard no limit understood.

Among our base iniquities
We sampled every drink about,
From glorious French vintages
To faro – Belgian beer – and stout,

And we tried those spirits even
Which people call redoubtable;
Our souls were in the seventh heaven,
Our bodies underneath the table.

Des paysages, des cités
Posaient pour nos yeux jamais las;
Nos belles curiosités
Eussent mangé tous les atlas.

Fleuves et monts, bronzes et marbres,
Les couchants d'or, l'aube magique,
L'Angleterre, mère des arbres,
Fille des beffrois, la Belgique,

La mer, terrible et douce au point, –
Brochaient sur le roman très cher
Que ne discontinuait point
Notre âme – et *quid* de notre chair? . . .

Le roman de vivre à deux hommes
Mieux que non pas d'époux modèles,
Chacun au tas versant des sommes
De sentiments forts et fidèles.

L'envie aux yeux de basilic
Censurait ce mode d'écot:
Nous dînions du blâme public
Et soupions du même fricot.

La misère aussi faisait rage
Par des fois dans le phalanstère:
On ripostait par le courage,
La joie et les pommes de terre.

Scandaleux sans savoir pourquoi
(Peut-être que c'était trop beau)
Mais notre couple restait coi
Comme deux bons porte-drapeau,

Coi dans l'orgueil d'être plus libres
Que les plus libres de ce monde,
Sourd aux gros mots de tous calibres,
Inaccessible au rire immonde.

Landscapes and cities lay revealed,
Like pictures, to our tireless eyes;
By curiosity compelled,
We would have eaten atlases.

River and mountain, statuaries,
Gold sunset and enchanted dawn,
England, the mother of all trees,
And Belgium, of belfries born,

The sea, gentle and terrible, –
All hastened the beloved romance
Not discontinued, truth to tell,
By both our souls – and flesh, perchance? . . .

The dear romance of man and man,
Living more blest than man and wife,
Each on the treasure heaping sums
Of feelings strong and loyal for life.

Envy, like a cockatrice,
Condemned our mode of reckoning:
We often dined on prejudice
And off the same stew we were breakfasting.

Poverty its havoc played
At times, in our community;
We replied with fortitude,
Potatoes, and new gaiety.

Scandalous, not knowing why
(Perhaps it was too glorious),
We two kept our serenity
Like colour-sergeants duteous,

Serene, and proud to be more free
Than the freest in the world,
Deaf to all kinds of injury,
Untouched by unclean stories told.

Nous avions laissé sans émoi
Tous impédiments dans Paris,
Lui quelques sots bernés, et moi
Certaine princesse Souris,

Une sotte qui tourna pire . . .
Puis soudain tomba notre gloire,
Tels, nous, des maréchaux d'empire
Déchus en brigands de la Loire,

Mais déchus volontairement !
C'était une permission,
Pour parler militairement,
Que notre séparation,

Permission sous nos semelles,
Et depuis combien de campagnes !
Pardonnâtes-vous aux femelles ?
Moi, j'ai peu revu ces compagnes,

Assez toutefois pour souffrir.
Ah, quel cœur faible que mon cœur !
Mais mieux vaut souffrir que mourir
Et surtout mourir de langueur.

On vous dit mort, vous. Que le Diable
Emporte avec qui la colporte
La nouvelle irrémédiable
Qui vient ainsi battre ma porte !

Je n'y veux rien croire. Mort, vous,
Toi, dieu parmi les demi-dieux !
Ceux qui le disent sont des fous.
Mort, mon grand péché radieux,

Tout ce passé brûlant encore
Dans mes veines et ma cervelle
Et qui rayonne et qui fulgore
Sur ma ferveur toujours nouvelle !

In Paris, very happily,
We'd left all our impediments,
He'd left a few scorned fools, and I
A certain Princess Pestilent,

An idiot who grew worse still . . .
Then suddenly our glory went:
Two Marshals, once imperial,
Now brigands without regiment.

But we had sunk of our own choice!
Leave of absence had been taken,
In the military phrase,
For our separation.

Our feet were winged, and leave we took
For countless expeditions!
Did you pardon womenfolk?
I've seen few such companions

Since then – enough for agony.
My heart's so weak I am undone!
Yet rather agonize than die,
Especially of dejection.

They say you're dead. You. May he die,
Whoever noises it abroad,
The message none can remedy,
Which beats, relentless, on my door.

My soul will not believe it. You are dead,
You, only god among the paladins?
Those who proclaim you dead are mad.
You dead, my radiant and glorious sin,

That burning past that still remains entire
And blazing in my blood and in my brain,
That incandescent past that flashes fire
Upon my fervour, ever new again!

Mort tout ce triomphe inouï
Retentissant sans frein ni fin
Sur l'air jamais évanoui
Que bat mon cœur qui fut divin !

Quoi, le miraculeux poème
Et la toute-philosophie,
Et ma patrie et ma bohème
Morts ? Allons donc ! tu vis ma vie !

It's dead, all that unheard-of victory
That echoes on without end or control,
And to one rhythm sings perpetually:
My heart that used to be celestial!

Oh, can it be? The poem heaven-born
And the philosophy definitive,
My country and my world Bohemian
All dead? It is not so! My life, you live!

Dédicaces   1890

A VILLIERS DE L'ISLE-ADAM

Tu nous fuis comme fuit le soleil sous la mer
Derrière un rideau lourd de pourpres léthargiques,
Las d'avoir splendi seul sur les ombres tragiques
De la terre sans verbe et de l'aveugle éther.

Tu pars, âme chrétienne on m'a dit résignée
Parce que tu savais que ton Dieu préparait
Une fête enfin claire à ton cœur sans secret,
Une amour toute flamme à ton amour ignée.

Nous restons pour encore un peu de temps ici,
Conservant ta mémoire en notre espoir transi,
Tels les mourants savourent l'huile du Saint-Chrême.

Villiers, sois envié comme il aurait fallu
Par tes frères impatients du jour suprême
Où saluer en toi la gloire d'un élu.

TO VILLIERS DE L'ISLE-ADAM

You leave us, like the sun beneath the sea,
Behind a veil heavy with purple sleep,
Weary of shining alone on the sad landscape
Of the wordless earth, the sky that cannot see.

They tell me, Christian soul, you go resigned,
Since you were certain that your God prepared
A welcome clear at last for your open heart,
A love all ardent for your love inflamed.

We linger yet a little while on earth,
Keeping your memory in our numbed faith,
As dying men savour Unction Extreme.

Oh, Villiers, be envied as you should
By brothers eager for the day supreme
When they hail you as an elect of God.

Bonheur 1891

«LA CATHÉDRALE EST MAJESTUEUSE...»

La cathédrale est majestueuse
Que j'imagine en pleine campagne
Sur quelque affluent de quelque Meuse
Non loin de l'Océan qu'il regagne,

L'Océan pas vu que je devine
Par l'air chargé de sels et d'arômes.
La croix est d'or dans la nuit divine
D'entre l'envol des tours et des dômes.

Des angélus font aux campaniles
Une couronne d'argent qui chante.
De blancs hiboux, au longs cris graciles,
Tournent sans fin de sorte charmante.

Des processions jeunes et claires
Vont et viennent de porches sans nombre,
Soie et perles de vivants rosaires,
Rogations pour de chers fruits d'ombre.

Ce n'est pas un rêve ni la vie,
C'est ma belle et ma chaste pensée,
Si vous voulez, ma philosophie,
Ma mort bien mienne ainsi déguisée.

'IN SPLENDOUR THE CATHEDRAL STANDS...'

In splendour the cathedral stands
– Or so I dream – deep in the countryside;
Nearby some tributary river winds
Towards the Ocean where it joins the tide,

The unseen Ocean I divine
From the salt-laden, aromatic air.
The cross in heavenly night doth golden shine,
Among the towers and domes that upward soar.

The Angelus make the bell-towers
A silver coronal that sings;
White owls, with long shrill cries, fly o'er,
Enchanted circle, ever on the wing.

Processions, young and bright and gay,
From doors innumerable come and go,
The silk and pearls of living rosaries,
Rogation for dear fruits that shadows know.

It is not dream nor yet reality,
It is my thought, candid and beautiful:
If you prefer it, my philosophy,
And my disguise for my own funeral.

«VOIX DE GABRIEL CHEZ L'HUMBLE MARIE...»

Voix de Gabriel
Chez l'humble Marie,
Cloches de Noël
Dans la nuit fleurie,
Siècles, célébrez
Mes sens délivrés.

Martyrs, troupe blanche,
Et les confesseurs,
Fruits d'or de la branche,
Vous, frères et sœurs,
Vierges dans la gloire,
Chantez ma victoire.

Les Saints ignorés,
Vertus qu'on méprise,
Qui nous sauverez
Par votre entremise,
Priez, que la foi
Demeure humble en moi.

Pécheurs, par le monde,
Qui vous repentez
Dans l'ardeur profonde
D'être rachetés,
Or je vous contemple,
Donnez-moi l'exemple.

'VOICE OF GABRIEL
TO MARY LOWLY...'

Voice of Gabriel
To Mary lowly,
Christmas bells
On night most holy,
And centuries,
Bless my senses freed.

Martyrs, white company,
Father-confessors,
Golden fruit of the tree,
You, brothers and sisters,
Virgins in glory,
Sing victory.

You Saints unknown,
Whom we set at naught,
By whose prayers alone
Is salvation bought,
Pray that piety
Stays meek in me.

Sinners everywhere,
Your repentance done,
In the longing for
Redemption,
I survey you now:
Oh, show me how.

Bonheur

Nature, animaux,
Eaux, plantes et pierres,
Vos simples travaux
Sont d'humbles prières.
Vous obéissez:
Pour Dieu, c'est assez.

Nature, animals,
Plants, water, stones,
Your simple toil
Is an orison.
You all obey:
That is God's way.

Chansons pour elle   1891

«JE SUIS PLUS PAUVRE QUE JAMAIS...»

Je suis plus pauvre que jamais
    Et que personne;
Mais j'ai ton cou gras, tes bras frais,
    Ta façon bonne
De faire l'amour, et le tour
    Leste et frivole
Et la caresse, nuit et jour,
    De ta parole.

Je suis riche de tes beaux yeux,
    De ta poitrine,
Nid follement voluptueux,
    Couche ivoirine
Où mon désir, las d'autre part,
    Se ravigore
Et pour d'autres ébats repart
    Plus brave encore ...

Sans doute tu ne m'aimes pas
    Comme je t'aime,
Je sais combien tu me trompas
    Jusqu'à l'extrême.
Que me fait puisque je ne vis
    Qu'en ton essence,
Et que tu tiens mes sens ravis
    Sous ta puissance?

'I AM POORER THAN EVER I WAS...'

I am poorer than ever I was
   Or anyone;
But I have your fat neck, sweet embrace,
   And your own
Happy way of love-making, your light
   Frivolous talk,
The caresses, by day and by night,
   Of words you speak.

I am wealthy in your fine eyes,
   And in your breast,
Couch wildly voluptuous,
   Ivory nest
Where my desire, elsewhere sated,
   Is renewed
To revel again, unabated,
   In plenitude . . .

I know that you do not love me
   As I love you,
I know quite well you've deceived me
   Constantly, too.
What's that to me since I only
   Live in you at all,
My senses, and all of me,
   Are in your thrall?

«JE FUS MYSTIQUE...»

Je fus mystique et je ne le suis plus,
(La femme m'aura repris tout entier)
Non sans garder des respects absolus
Pour l'idéal qu'il fallut renier.

Mais la femme m'a repris tout entier!

J'allais priant le Dieu de mon enfance
(Aujourd'hui c'est toi qui m'as à genoux).
J'étais plein de foi, de blanche espérance,
De charité sainte aux purs feux si doux.

Mais aujourd'hui tu m'as à tes genoux!

La femme, par toi, redevient LE maître,
Un maître tout-puissant et tyrannique,
Mais qu'insidieux! feignant de tout permettre
Pour en arriver à tel but satanique...

Ô le temps béni quand j'étais ce mystique!

'I WAS A MYSTIC...'

I was a mystic, I am so no more,
(Woman has conquered all of me again)
Though I keep the complete respect I had before
For the ideal that I could not maintain.

But woman has conquered all of me again!

I went about praying the God of childhood times
(Today it's you alone who make me kneel).
I was full of faith, of hope as yet undimmed,
Holy charity, its fire celestial.

But today it's you alone who make me kneel!

Woman, through you, becomes again THE lord,
A lord omnipotent, tyrannical,
Who cunningly pretends all to accord
To gain a purpose diabolical . . .

Oh, blessed time when I was mystical!

Odes en son honneur   1893

«JE NE SUIS PAS JALOUX
DE TON PASSÉ, CHÉRIE...»

Je ne suis pas jaloux de ton passé, chérie,
Et même je t'en aime et t'en admire mieux.
Il montre ton grand cœur et la gloire inflétrie
D'un amour tendre et fort autant qu'impérieux.

Car tu n'eus peur ni de la mort ni de la vie,
Et, jusqu'à cet automne fier répercuté
Vers les jours orageux de ta prime beauté,
Ton beau sanglot, honneur sublime, t'a suivie.

Ton beau sanglot que ton beau rire condolait
Comme un frère plus mâle, et ces deux bons génies
T'ont sacrée à mes yeux de vertus infinies
Dont mon amour à moi, tout fier, se prévalait

Et se targue pour t'adorer au sens mystique:
Consolations, vœux, respects, en même temps
Qu'humbles caresses et qu'hommages ex-votants
De ma chair à ce corps vaillant, temple héroïque

Où tant de passions comme en un Panthéon,
Rancœurs, pardons, fureurs et la sainte luxure
Tinrent leur culte, respectant la forme pure
Et le galbe puissant profanés par Phaon.

Pense à Phaon pour l'oublier dans mon étreinte
Plus douce et plus fidèle, amant d'après-midi,
D'extrême après-midi, mais non pas attiédi,
Que me voici, tout plein d'extases et de crainte.

'I AM NOT JEALOUS
OF YOUR PAST, MY DEAR...'

I am not jealous of your past, my dear.
It even makes me love, admire you more.
It shows your great heart, constant harbinger
Of love impetuous, strong as before.

For you were not afraid of death or life,
And, unto this proud autumn echoing
From your tempestuous days, your beauty's spring,
You've brought your fine cry, prize superlative.

Your fine cry, soon consoled by your fine laugh,
Like a more manly brother, deities
That crown you with countless virtues in my eyes
And, proudly, I enjoy them in my love,

And pride myself on worship mystical,
Give you respect, vows, consolation
As well as humble caresses, the oblation
Of my flesh to this flesh heroical

Where countless passions in a Pantheon,
Rancours, pardons, rages, and blest desire
Professed their cult, the pure form to admire,
The mighty curves profaned once by Phaon.

Think of Phaon to forget him in my embrace
More faithful and gentle, lover of afternoon,
Extreme afternoon, but not without its sun,
For here I am, full of fear and ecstasies.

Va, je t'aime . . . mieux que l'autre : il faut l'oublier.
Toi : souris-moi entre deux confidences,
Amazone blessée ès belles imprudences
Qui se réveille au sein d'un vieux brave écuyer.

I love you . . . more than he did: forget him. Come,
At least between two secrets smile at me,
Amazon hurt by your fine temerity
Who wakes again in the arms of a faithful groom.

Le Livre posthume   1893-4

FRAGMENTS (I)

Dis, sérieusement, lorsque je serai mort,
Plein de toi, sens, esprit, âme, et dans la prunelle
Ton image à jamais pour la nuit éternelle;
Au cœur tout ce passé tendre et farouche, sort

Divin, l'incomparable entre les jouissances
Immenses de ma vie excessive, ô toi, dis,
Pense parfois à moi qui ne pensais jadis
Qu'à t'aimer, t'adorer de toutes les puissances

D'un être fait exprès pour toi seule t'aimer,
Toi seule te servir et vivre pour toi seule
Et mourir en toi seule. Et puis quand belle aïeule
Tu penseras à moi, garde-toi d'exhumer

Mes jours de jalousie et mes nuits d'humeur noire:
Plutôt évoque l'abandon entre tes mains
De tout moi, tout au bon présent, aux chers demains,
Et qu'une bénédiction de la mémoire

M'absolve, et soit mon guide en les sombres chemins.

FRAGMENTS (I)

Answer me truly: when I go, at last,
Full of you, senses, spirit, soul, my sight
Holding your image for eternal night,
In my heart all this fierce and tender past,

Fortune divine, which set every delight,
Every extravagance of mine at naught:
Oh, then, think sometimes of me, who once thought
Only to love, adore you with the might

Of one created to love you alone,
Serve you alone, and live, alone, for you
And die only in you. Recall me, too,
When you are old, but leave within my tomb

My days of anger, nights of misery.
Rather recall I gave into your hands
My whole self: present, future, your commands.
And may a blessing of the memory

Absolve me, guide me through the darker lands.

DERNIER ESPOIR

Il est un arbre au cimetière
Poussant en pleine liberté,
Non planté par un deuil dicté, –
Qui flotte au long d'une humble pierre.

Sur cet arbre, été comme hiver,
Un oiseau vient qui chante clair
Sa chanson tristement fidèle.
Cet arbre et cet oiseau c'est nous:

Toi le souvenir, moi l'absence
Que le temps – qui passe – recense . . .
Ah, vivre encore à tes genoux!

Ah, vivre encor! Mais quoi, ma belle,
Le néant est mon froid vainqueur . . .
Du moins, dis, je vis dans ton cœur?

LAST HOPE

In the graveyard is a tree
Which in utter freedom grows,
Not set there by dictated woes, –
Beside a stone it waves in elegy.

Summer and winter to it bring
A melancholy bird which sings
Its song of love so sad and clear.
We are that faithful bird, that tree:

You are remembrance, I the person gone,
The absence verified by passing time . . .
Oh, still to live, and still your zealot be!

Oh, still to live! Alas, my dear,
Oblivion is my cold conqueror . . .
At least, say I live in you evermore?

INDEX OF TITLES

INDEX OF FIRST LINES

Je ne suis pas jaloux de ton passé, chérie, 236
　　I am not jealous of your past, my dear, 237
Je ne veux plus aimer que ma mère Marie, 138
　　My mother Mary shall be all I love, 139
Je suis l'Empire à la fin de la décadence, 180
　　I am the Empire late in the decadence, 181
Je suis plus pauvre que jamais, 230
　　I am poorer than ever I was, 231
Je suis venu, calme orphelin, 152
　　I came, serene and fatherless, 153
Je vois un groupe sur la mer, 184
　　I see a vision on the sea, 185

L'abbé divague. – Et toi, marquis, 62
　　The abbé's rambling. – Let me tell, 63
La cathédrale est majestueuse, 222
　　In splendour the cathedral stands, 223
La dure épreuve va finir, 96
　　The harsh ordeal is going to end, 97
La lune blanche, 92
　　The silver moon, 93
La lune est rouge au brumeux horizon, 46
　　The moon lies roseate upon the mist, 47
La mer est plus belle, 162
　　The sea's lovelier, 163
Le ciel est, par-dessus le toit, 156
　　The sky is high above the roof, 157
Le ciel si pâle et les arbres si grêles, 66
　　The sky so colourless, the trees so thin, 67
Le foyer, la lueur étroite de la lampe, 100
　　The hearth, the lamp, the narrow-circled light, 101
Le piano que baise une main frêle, 110
　　The piano kissed by a frail hand, 111
Les chères mains qui furent miennes, 130
　　Dear hands which used to be my own, 131
Les courses furent intrépides, 208
　　The travels were adventurous, 209
Les faux beaux jours ont lui tout le jour, ma pauvre âme, 126
　　The false fine days have shone all day, my soul, 127

More about Penguins and Pelicans

Penguinews, which appears every month, contains details of all the new books issued by Penguins as they are published. From time to time it is supplemented by *Penguins in Print,* which is a complete list of all titles available. (There are some five thousand of these.)

A specimen copy of *Penguinews* will be sent to you free on request. For a year's issues (including the complete lists) please send 50p if you live in the British Isles, or 75p if you live elsewhere. Just write to Dept EP, Penguin Books Ltd, Harmondsworth, Middlesex, enclosing a cheque or postal order, and your name will be added to the mailing list.

In the U.S.A.: For a complete list of books available from Penguin in the United States write to Dept CS, Penguin Books Inc., 7110 Ambassador Road, Baltimore, Maryland 21207.

In Canada: For a complete list of books available from Penguin in Canada write to Penguin Books Canada Ltd, 41 Steelcase Road West, Markham, Ontario.

Poet to Poet

The response of one poet to the work of another can be doubly
illuminating. In each volume of this new Penguin series a modern
poet presents his own edition of the work of a British or
American poet of the past. By their choice of poet, by their
selection of verses, and by the personal and critical reactions they
express in their introductions, the poets of today thus provide an
intriguing insight into themselves and their own work whilst
reviving interest in poetry they have particularly admired.

Already published:

Crabbe *by C. Day Lewis*
Henryson *by Hugh MacDiarmid*
George Herbert *by W. H. Auden*
Ben Jonson *by Thom Gunn*
Pope *by Peter Levi*
Shelley *by Kathleen Raine*
Tennyson *by Kingsley Amis*
Whitman *by Robert Creeley*
Wordsworth *by Lawrence Durrell*

Future volumes will include:

Arnold *by Stephen Spender*
Keats *by Ian Hamilton*
Marvell *by William Empson*
Swinburne *by I. A. Richards*